Artificial Intelligence for IoT Cookbook

Over 70 recipes for building AI solutions for smart homes, industrial IoT, and smart cities

Michael Roshak

BIRMINGHAM - MUMBAI

Artificial Intelligence for IoT Cookbook

Group Product Manager: Kunal Parikh
Publishing Product Manager: Devika Battike
Senior Editor: David Sugarman
Content Development Editor: Athikho Sapuni Rishana
Technical Editor: Manikandan Kurup
Copy Editor: Safis Editing
Project Coordinator: Aishwarya Mohan
Proofreader: Safis Editing
Indexer: Rekha Nair
Production Designer: Nilesh Mohite

First published: March 2021

Production reference: 1040221

Published by Packt Publishing Ltd.
Livery Place
35 Livery Street
Birmingham
B3 2PB, UK.

ISBN 978-1-83898-198-3

www.packt.com

Contributors

About the author

Michael Roshak is a cloud architect and strategist who has gained extensive subject matter expertise in enterprise cloud transformation programs and infrastructure modernization through designing and deploying cloud-oriented solutions and architectures. He is responsible for providing strategic advisory services for cloud adoption, consultative technical sales, and driving broad cloud services consumption with highly strategic accounts across multiple industries.

About the reviewer

Va Barbosa is a software engineer with the Qiskit Community at IBM, focused on building open source tools and creating educational content for developers, researchers, students, and educators in the field of quantum computing. Previously, Va was a developer advocate with the Center for Open Source Data and AI Technologies, where he helped developers to discover and make use of data science and machine learning technologies. He is fueled by his passion to help others and guided by his enthusiasm for open source technology.

Table of Contents

Preface

Artificial intelligence (AI) is rapidly finding practical applications across a wide variety of industry verticals, and the **Internet of Things (IoT)** is one of them. Developers are looking for ways to make IoT devices smarter and to make users' lives easier. With this AI cookbook, you'll learn how to implement smart analytics using IoT data to gain insights, predict outcomes, and make informed decisions, along with covering advanced AI techniques that facilitate analytics and learning in various IoT applications.

Using a recipe-based approach, the book will take you through essential processes such as data collection, data analysis, modeling, statistics and monitoring, and deployment. You'll use real-life datasets from smart homes, industrial IoT, and smart devices to train and evaluate simple and complex models and make predictions using trained models. Later chapters will take you through the key challenges faced while implementing machine learning, deep learning, and other AI techniques such as **natural language processing (NLP)**, computer vision, and embedded machine learning to build smart IoT systems. In addition to this, you'll learn how to deploy models and improve their performance with ease.

By the end of this book, you'll be able to package and deploy end-to-end AI apps and apply best practice solutions to common IoT problems.

Who this book is for

If you're an IoT practitioner looking to incorporate AI techniques to build smart IoT solutions without having to trawl through a lot of AI theory, this AI IoT book is for you. Data scientists and AI developers who want to build IoT-focused AI solutions will also find this book useful. Knowledge of the Python programming language and basic IoT concepts is required to grasp the concepts covered in this AI book effectively.

What this book covers

Chapter 1, *Setting Up the IoT and AI Environment*, will focus on getting the right environment set up for success. You will learn how to choose a device that meets your needs for AI, whether that model needs to be on the edge or in the cloud. You will also learn how to securely communicate with modules within a device, other devices, or the cloud. Finally, you will set up a way to ingest data in the cloud and then set up Spark and AI tools to perform analysis of data, train models, and run machine learning models at scale.

Chapter 2, *Handling Data*, talks about the basics of ensuring that data in any format can be used by data scientists effectively.

Chapter 3, *Machine Learning for IoT*, will discuss using machine learning models such as logistic regression and decision trees to solve common IoT issues such as classifying medical results, detecting unsafe drivers, and classifying chemical readings.

Chapter 4, *Deep Learning for Predictive Maintenance*, will focus on various classification techniques to enable IoT devices to be smart devices.

Chapter 5, *Anomaly Detection*, will explain how when alarm detection does not classify a particular issue, it can lead to the discovery of issues, and how if a device is acting in an anomalous way, you might want to send out a repair worker to examine the device.

Chapter 6, *Computer Vision*, will discuss implementing computer vision in the cloud as well as on edge devices such as NVIDIA Jetson Nano.

Chapter 7, *NLP and Bots for a Self-Ordering Kiosk*, will discuss using NLP and using bots to enable interaction with users ordering foods at a restaurant kiosk.

Chapter 8, *Optimizing with Microcontrollers and Pipelines*, will discuss how reinforcement learning can be used with a smart traffic intersection to make traffic light decisions that decrease the wait time at traffic lights and allow traffic to flow better.

Chapter 9, *Deploying to the Edge*, will discuss various ways of applying pre-trained machine learning models to an edge device. This chapter will discuss IoT Edge in detail. Deploying is an important part of the AI pipeline. This chapter will also talk about deploying machine learning models to web applications and mobile using TensorFlow.js and ONNX.

To get the most out of this book

Readers should have a basic understanding of software development. This book uses the Python, C, Java languages. A basic understanding of how to install libraries and packages in these languages as well as basic coding concepts such as arrays and loops will be helpful. A few websites that can help you brush up on the basics of different languages are:

- https://www.learnpython.org/
- https://www.learnjavaonline.org/
- https://www.learn-c.org/

To get the most out of this book a basic understanding of machine learning principles will be beneficial. The hardware used in this book are off the shelf sensors and common IoT development kits and can be purchased from sites such as Adafruit.com and Amazon.com. Most of the code is portable across devices. Device code written in Python can be easily ported to a variety of microprocessors such as a Raspberry Pi, Nvidia Jetson, Lotte Panda, or sometimes even a PC. While code written in C can be ported to a variety of microcontrollers such as the ESP32, ESP8266, and Arduino. Code written in Java can be ported to any android device such as a tablet or phone.

This book uses Databricks for some of the experiments. Databricks has a free version at https://community.cloud.databricks.com.

If you are using the digital version of this book, we advise you to type the code yourself or access the code via the GitHub repository (link available in the next section). Doing so will help you avoid any potential errors related to the copying and pasting of code.

Download the example code files

You can download the example code files for this book from GitHub at https://github.com/PacktPublishing/Artificial-Intelligence-for-IoT-Cookbook. In case there's an update to the code, it will be updated on the existing GitHub repository.

We also have other code bundles from our rich catalog of books and videos available at https://github.com/PacktPublishing/. Check them out!

Download the color images

We also provide a PDF file that has color images of the screenshots/diagrams used in this book. You can download it here:
https://static.packt-cdn.com/downloads/9781838981983_ColorImages.pdf.

Conventions used

There are a number of text conventions used throughout this book.

`CodeInText`: Indicates code words in text, database table names, folder names, filenames, file extensions, pathnames, dummy URLs, user input, and Twitter handles. Here is an example: "This will give you a list of the running containers. Then, open the `/data` folder."

A block of code is set as follows:

```
import numpy as np
import torch
from torch import nn
from torch import optim
import torch.nn.functional as F
from torchvision import datasets, transforms, models
from torch.utils.data.sampler import SubsetRandomSampler
```

Any command-line input or output is written as follows:

```
cd jetson-inference
mkdir build
cd build
```

Bold: Indicates a new term, an important word, or words that you see onscreen. For example, words in menus or dialog boxes appear in the text like this. Here is an example: "Click on the **New project** tile. Then, fill out the **Create new project** wizard."

Warnings or important notes appear like this.

Tips and tricks appear like this.

Sections

In this book, you will find several headings that appear frequently (*Getting ready, How to do it..., How it works..., There's more...*, and *See also*).

To give clear instructions on how to complete a recipe, use these sections as follows:

Getting ready

This section tells you what to expect in the recipe and describes how to set up any software or any preliminary settings required for the recipe.

How to do it...

This section contains the steps required to follow the recipe.

How it works...

This section usually consists of a detailed explanation of what happened in the previous section.

There's more...

This section consists of additional information about the recipe in order to make you more knowledgeable about the recipe.

See also

This section provides helpful links to other useful information for the recipe.

Get in touch

Feedback from our readers is always welcome.

General feedback: If you have questions about any aspect of this book, mention the book title in the subject of your message and email us at customercare@packtpub.com.

Errata: Although we have taken every care to ensure the accuracy of our content, mistakes do happen. If you have found a mistake in this book, we would be grateful if you would report this to us. Please visit www.packtpub.com/support/errata, selecting your book, clicking on the Errata Submission Form link, and entering the details.

Piracy: If you come across any illegal copies of our works in any form on the Internet, we would be grateful if you would provide us with the location address or website name. Please contact us at copyright@packt.com with a link to the material.

If you are interested in becoming an author: If there is a topic that you have expertise in and you are interested in either writing or contributing to a book, please visit authors.packtpub.com.

Reviews

Please leave a review. Once you have read and used this book, why not leave a review on the site that you purchased it from? Potential readers can then see and use your unbiased opinion to make purchase decisions, we at Packt can understand what you think about our products, and our authors can see your feedback on their book. Thank you!

For more information about Packt, please visit packt.com.

Setting Up the IoT and AI Environment

1

The **Internet of Things** (**IoT**) and **artificial intelligence** (**AI**) are leading to a dramatic impact on people's lives. Industries such as medicine are being revolutionized by wearable sensors that can monitor patients after they leave the hospital. **Machine learning** (**ML**) used on industrial devices is leading to better monitoring and less downtime with techniques such as anomaly detection, predictive maintenance, and prescriptive actions.

Building an IoT device capable of delivering results relies on gathering the right information. This book gives recipes that support the end-to-end IoT/ML life cycle. The next chapter has recipes for making sure that devices have the right sensors and the data is the best it can be for ML outcomes. Tools such as explanatory factor analysis and data collection design are used.

This chapter will cover the following topics:

- Choosing a device
- Setting up Databricks

The following recipes will be covered:

- Setting up IoT Hub
- Setting up an IoT Edge device
- Deploying ML modules to Edge devices
- Setting up Kafka
- Installing ML libraries on Databricks

Choosing a device

Before starting with the classic recipe-by-recipe formatting of a cookbook, we'll start by covering a couple of base topics. Choosing the right hardware sets the stage for AI. Working with IoT means working with constraints. Using ML in the cloud is often a cost-effective solution as long as the data is small. Image, video, and sound data will often bog down networks. Worse yet, if you are using a cellular network, it can be highly expensive. The adage *there is no money in hardware* refers to the fact that most of the money made from IoT comes from the selling of services, not from producing expensive devices.

Dev kits

Often, companies have their devices designed by electrical engineers. This is a cost-effective option. Custom boards do not have extra components, such as unnecessary Bluetooth or extra USB ports. However, predicting CPU and RAM requirements of an ML model at board design time is difficult. Starter kits can be useful tools to use until the hardware requirements are understood. The following boards are among the most widely adopted boards on the market:

- Manifold 2-C with NVIDIA TX2
- The i.MX series
- LattePanda
- Raspberry Pi Class
- Arduino
- ESP8266

They are often used as a scale of functionality. A Raspberry Pi Class device, for example, would struggle with custom vision applications but would do great for audio or general ML applications. One determining factor for many data scientists is the programming language. The ESP8266 and Arduino need to be programmed in a low-level language such as C or C++, while devices such as Raspberry Pi Class or above can be programmed in any language.

Different devices come at different prices and functionalities. Devices that are Raspberry Pi Class or above can handle ML running on the Edge, reducing cloud cost but increasing the cost of the device. Deciding on whether you are billing your customers with a one-time price for the device or a subscription model may help you determine what type of device you need.

Manifold 2-C with NVIDIA TX2

The NVIDIA Jetson is one of the best choices for running complex ML models such as real-time video on the Edge. The NVIDIA Jetson comes with a built-in NVIDIA GPU. The Manifold version of the product is designed to fit onto a DJI drone and perform tasks such as image recognition or self-flying. The only downside to running NVIDIA Jetson is its use of the ARM64 architecture. ARM64 does not work well with TensorFlow, although other libraries such as PyTorch work fine on ARM64. The Manifold retails for $500, which makes it a high-price option, but this is often necessary when doing real-time ML on the Edge:

Price	Typical Models	Use Cases
$500	Re-enforcement learning, computer vision	Self-flying drones, robotics

The i.MX series

The i.MX series of chips is open source and boasts impressive RAM and CPU capabilities. The open design helps engineers build boards easily. The i.MX series uses Freescale semiconductors. Freescale semiconductors have guaranteed production life runs of 10 through 15 years, which means the board design will be stable for years. The i.MX 6 can range from $200 to $300 in cost and can handle CPU-intensive tasks easily, such as object recognition in live streaming video:

Price	Typical Models	Use Cases
$200+	Computer vision, NLP	Sentiment analysis, face recognition, object recognition, voice recognition

LattePanda

Single Board Computers (**SBCs**) such as the LattePanda are capable of running heavy sensor workloads. These devices can often run Windows or Linux. Like the i.MX series, they are capable of running object recognition on the device; however, the frame rate for recognizing objects can be slow:

Price	Typical Models	Use Cases
$100+	Face detection, voice recognition, high-speed Edge models	Audio-enabled kiosk, high-frequency heart monitoring

Raspberry Pi Class

Raspberry Pis are a standard starter kit for IoT. With their $35 price tag, they give you a lot of capability for the cost: they can run ML on the Edge with containers. They have a Linux or IoT Core operating system, which allows the easy plugging and playing of components and a community of developers building similar platform tools. Although Raspberry Pi Class devices are capable of handling most ML tasks, they tend to have performance issues on some of the more intensive tasks, such as video recognition:

Price	Typical Models	Use Cases
$35	Decision trees, artificial neural networks, anomaly detection	Smart home, industrial IoT

Arduino

At $15, the Arduino is a cost-effective solution. Arduino is supported by a large community and uses the Arduino language, a set of C/C++ functions. If you need to run ML models on an Arduino device, it is possible to package ML models built on popular frameworks such as PyTorch into the **Embedded Learning Library** (**ELL**). The ELL allows ML models to be deployed on the device without needing the overhead of a large operating system. Porting ML models using ELL or TensorFlow Lite can be challenging due to the limited memory and compute capacity of the Arduino:

Price	Typical Models	Use Cases
$15	Linear regression	Sensor reading classification

ESP8266

At under $5, devices such as the ESP8266 and smaller represent a class of devices that take data in and transmit it to the cloud for ML evaluations. Besides being inexpensive, they are also often low-power devices, so they can be powered by solar power, network power, or a long-life battery:

Price	Typical Models	Use Cases
$5 or below	In the cloud only	In the cloud only

Setting up Databricks

Processing large amounts of data is not possible on a single computer. That is where distributed systems such as Spark (made by Databricks) come in. Spark allows you to parallelize large workloads over many computers.

Spark was developed to help solve the **Netflix Prize**, which had a $1 million prize for the team that made the best recommendation engine. Spark uses distributed computing to wrangle large and complex datasets. There are distributed Python equivalent libraries, such as Koalas, which is a distributed equivalent of pandas. Spark also supports analytics and feature engineering that requires a large amount of compute and memory, such as graph theory problems. Spark has two modes: a batch mode for training large datasets and a streaming mode for scoring data in near real time.

IoT data tends to be large and imbalanced. A device may have 10 years of data showing it is running in normal conditions and only a few records showing it needs to be shut down immediately to prevent damage. The value of Databricks in IoT is twofold. The first is working with data and training models. Working with data at the terabyte and petabyte scale can overwhelm a single machine. Databricks solves this with its ability to scale out. The second is its streaming capabilities. ML models can be run in the cloud in near real time. Messages can then be pushed back down to the device.

Setting up Databricks is fairly straightforward. You can either go to your cloud provider and sign up for an account in the portal or sign up for the free community edition. If you are taking your product to production, then you should definitely sign up with Azure, AWS, or Google Cloud.

IoT and ML are fundamentally a big data problem. A device may send telemetry for years before it sends telemetry that would indicate an issue with the device. Searching through millions or billions of records to find the few records that are needed can be challenging from a data management perspective. Therefore, optimal data storage is key.

Storing data

Today, there are tools that make it easy to work with large amounts of data. There are a few things to remember though. There are optimal ways of storing data at scale that can make dealing with large datasets easier.

Working with data, the type of large datasets that come from IoT devices can be prohibitively expensive for many companies. Storing data in Delta Lake, for example, can give the user a 340-times performance boost over accessing the data over JSON. The next three sections will introduce three storage methods that can cut down a data analytics job from weeks to hours.

Parquet

Parquet is one of the most common file formats in big data. Parquet's columnar storage format allows it to store highly compressed data. Its advantage is that it takes up less space on the hard disk and takes up less network bandwidth, making it ideal for loading into a DataFrame. Parquet ingestion into Spark has been benchmarked at 34 times the speed of JSON.

Avro

The Avro format is a popular storage format for IoT. While it does not have the high compression ratio that Parquet does, it is less compute expensive to store data because it uses a row-level data storage schema. Avro is a common format for streaming data such as IoT Hub or Kafka.

Delta Lake

Delta Lake is an open source project released by Databricks in 2019. It stores files in Parquet. In addition, it is able to keep track of data check-ins, enabling the data scientist to look at data as it existed at a given time. This can be useful when trying to determine why accuracy in a particular ML model drifted. It also keeps metadata about the data, giving it a 10-times performance increase over standard Parquet for analytics workloads.

While considerations are given to both choosing a device and setting up Databricks, the rest of this chapter will follow a modular, recipe-based format.

Setting up IoT Hub

Developing IoT solutions can be complicated. There are many issues to deal with, such as ML, Edge deployments, security, monitoring device state, and ingesting telemetry in the cloud. Cloud providers such as Azure provide a ready-made solution that can have components such as data storage and cloud-to-device messages built in.

In this recipe, we are going to set up IoT Hub in Azure for an IoT Edge device that will be doing ML calculations on the Edge.

Getting ready

Before using IoT Hub, you need to have a device and an Azure subscription. There is a free trial subscription available if you do not already have one. You will also need some sort of device.

How to do it...

To set up IoT Hub, the first thing you will need is a resource group. Resource groups are like folders on Windows or macOS. They allow you to place all of the resources for a particular project in the same location. The resource groups icon is in the **Favorites** menu in the left panel of the Azure portal:

The following is what we need to do:

1. Select **Create a resource**. From there, the wizard will take you through the steps to create a resource group.
2. Then, click on the + icon at the top to create an IoT Hub instance.
3. In the search box, type in `IoT Hub`. The wizard will take you through how to set up IoT Hub.

One important thing to note on the Scale page is you will want to select the S1 or higher pricing tier. The S1 tier gives you bidirectional communication with the device and also enables you to use advanced features such as dice twins and the ability to push ML models to Edge devices.

How it works...

IoT Hub is a platform developed specifically for IoT. Issues that affect IoT, such as unreliable communication, are handled through mechanisms such as **Advanced Message Queuing Protocol (AMQP)** and **Message Queuing Telemetry Transport (MQTT)**. IoT Hub has a rich ecosystem of tools to help IoT developers, such as device twins, cloud-to-device messages, a device security center, Kubernetes integration, and a marketplace for Edge modules.

Setting up an IoT Edge device

In this recipe, we're going to set up an IoT Edge device that can communicate with IoT Hub and also receive new ML containers that it can use to perform ML evaluations on the device.

IoT Edge devices have advantages over traditional IoT devices. The main advantage is their ability to update **over the air (OTA)**. By using containers, models can be deployed easily without having to worry about bricking the device.

Getting ready

Before you create an IoT Edge device, make sure that your device is supported by IoT Edge. Some device architectures, such as ARM64, are not. Next, make sure your IoT Hub instance from the previous recipe is up and running. The IoT Edge runtime must be installed on your device. For the sake of this tutorial, we will assume that the user has a Raspberry Pi Class device.

How to do it...

To set up an IoT Edge device, you will need to set up both the cloud and device side. The IoT device needs a place in the cloud to send its information. This recipe has two parts. The first part is configuring the IoT Edge device in IoT Hub. The second is configuring the device to talk to the cloud.

Configuring an IoT Edge device (cloud side)

The steps are as follows:

1. In the IoT Hub blade, select **IoT Edge**.
2. Click on the **+ Add an IoT Edge device** button. This will take you to the **Add IoT Edge device** wizard.
3. Give your device a unique device ID and select **Save**.
4. A new device will be displayed in the middle of the screen. Click on that device and copy its primary connection string:

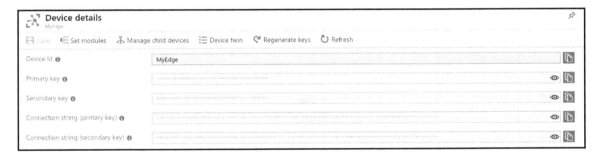

The next section explains getting a device to talk to the cloud. To do this, you will need the device connection string. The device connection string can be found in the device properties section. Click on the device you want the connection string from and copy the connection string.

Configuring an IoT Edge device (device side)

The first thing to do is to install Moby. Moby is a scaled-down version of Docker. Docker allows you to push Edge modules down to the device. These models can be data-collected modules from sensors and they can also be ML modules. The steps are as follows:

1. Download and install the Moby engine on the device:

```
curl -L https://aka.ms/moby-engine-armhf-latest -o moby_engine.deb
&& sudo dpkg -i ./moby_engine.deb
```

2. Download and install the Moby CLI:

```
curl -L https://aka.ms/moby-cli-armhf-latest -o moby_cli.deb &&
sudo dpkg -i ./moby_cli.deb
```

3. Fix the installation:

```
sudo apt-get install -f
```

4. Install the IoT Edge security manager:

```
curl -L https://aka.ms/libiothsm-std-linux-armhf-latest -o
libiothsm-std.deb && sudo dpkg -i ./libiothsm-std.deb
```

5. Install the security daemon:

```
curl -L https://aka.ms/iotedged-linux-armhf-latest -o iotedge.deb
&& sudo dpkg -i ./iotedge.deb
```

6. Fix the installation:

```
sudo apt-get install -f
```

7. Edit the config file for the Edge device. If you do not have nano already installed on your device, you may need to install it. nano is a command line-based text editor that will work over SSH:

```
sudo nano /etc/iotedge/config.yaml
```

8. In the `nano` text editor, find the device connection string. Then, paste the device connection string you copied from the IoT Hub portal into the "`<ADD DEVICE CONNECTION STRING HERE>`" section:

```
provisioning:
  source: "manual"
  device_connection_string: "<ADD DEVICE CONNECTION STRING HERE>"
```

From there, you need to save and exit `nano`. To do this, press *Ctrl + X*. The terminal will have a saving confirmation message. Press *Y* to confirm and save. Then, it is time to restart the service on the device to pick up the changes.

9. Restart the Edge service using the following command:

```
sudo systemctl restart iotedge
```

How it works...

In this recipe, we've created a device in the cloud that has a specific key for that device. This is part of a security measure where each device has its own unique key for a device. If a device becomes compromised, it can be shut off.

We then added the IoT Edge SDK to the device and connected it to the cloud. At this point, the device is fully connected to the cloud and is ready to receive ML models and send its telemetry to the cloud. The next step is to deploy Edge modules to the device. These Edge modules are dockerized containers that can access sensors on the device and send telemetry to the cloud or run a trained model.

Deploying ML modules to Edge devices

Docker is the primary method of deployment for IoT devices. Docker allows you to create and test containers locally and deploy them to edge devices. Docker files can be specially scripted to deploy in various chip architectures such as x86 and ARM. In this recipe, we're going to walk through creating an IoT Edge module with ML libraries deployed from the cloud.

Getting ready

To create an IoT Edge module, first install Visual Studio Code. After Visual Studio Code is up and running, install the Azure IoT Edge extension. This can be done by finding the extension icon (⊞) in the side panel of Visual Studio Code. In the extension search bar, search for `azure iot edge` and install the extension:

After installing the extension, Visual Studio Code now has a wizard that can create an IoT Edge deployment. With a few modifications, it can be configured to deploy an ML model.

How to do it...

The steps for this recipe are as follows:

1. In Visual Studio Code, press *Ctrl* + *Shift* + *P* to bring up the command window and find **Azure IoT Edge: New IoT Edge Solution**:

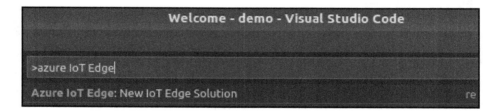

2. Select a location for your code.
3. Enter a solution name.
4. Choose a language. For the purpose of this book, we will be using Python as our language.
5. Create a module name.
6. Select a local port for running your code locally.

How it works...

After completing the wizard, you should see something in your Visual Studio Code explorer that looks like the following:

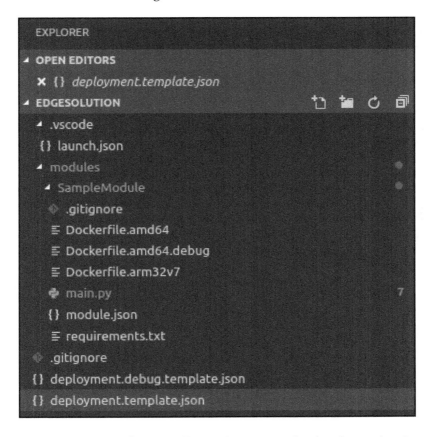

Let's explore what was created for you. The main entry point for the project is `main.py`. `main.py` has a sample to help make the development time faster. To deploy `main.py`, you will use the `deployment.template.json` file. Right-clicking on `deployment.template.json` brings up a menu that has an option to create a deployment manifest. In the `modules` folder, there is a sample module with three Docker files for ARM32, AMD64, and AMD64 in debug mode. These are the currently supported chip set architectures. `Dockerfile.arm32v7` is the architecture that is supported on Raspberry Pi v3.

To make sure you build ARM32 containers and not AMD64 containers, go into the `module.json` file and remove any references to other Docker files. For example, the following has three Docker references:

```
platforms": {
      "amd64": "./Dockerfile.amd64",
      "amd64.debug": "./Dockerfile.amd64.debug",
      "arm32v7": "./Dockerfile.arm32v7"
    }
```

After removing two Docker references that are not used, the new file should now look as follows:

```
platforms": {
"arm32v7": "./Dockerfile.arm32v7"
}
```

There's more...

To install TensorFlow, which is an ML library, Keras, which is an abstraction layer on top of TensorFlow that makes it easier to program, and h5py, which is a serialization layer that allows you to serialize and deserialize TensorFlow models, go to the target Docker container, then go into the `requirements.txt` file and install the libraries by inserting the following:

```
tensorflow
keras
h5py
```

Setting up Kafka

Kafka is an open source project that is inexpensive at scale, can execute ML models with millisecond latency, and has a multi-topic pub/sub model. There are several ways to set up Kafka. It is an open source project, so you can download the Kafka project and run Zookeeper and Kafka locally. Confluent, the parent company of Kafka, has a paid service that offers many additional features, such as dashboards and KSQL. They are available in Azure, AWS, and Google Cloud as a managed service and also, you can run Kafka as a dockerized container for development use.

One downside about using Kafka is that there is a lot of additional overhead to do to make it a good IoT project. Kafka, for example, is not secure by default. Security is handled through a series of plugins both on the device side through x.509 certificates and on the cloud side through **Lightweight Directory Access Protocol (LDAP)**, Ranger, or Kerberos plugins. Deploying ML models is also not trivial. Any ML libraries need to be converted into something a Java compiler can use. TensorFlow has TensorFlow for Java but many ML libraries are not available in Java.

Getting ready

In this example, we will be using Confluent Kafka in `docker-compose`. You will need to have Git, Docker, and `docker-compose` installed on your computer to run this recipe. To add ML models to Kafka streams, you will need to use a platform that runs on Java, such as H2O or TensorFlow.

How to do it...

The steps for this recipe are as follows:

1. Clone the repo:

   ```
   git clone https://github.com/confluentinc/cp-all-in-on
   ```

2. Run `docker-compose`:

   ```
   docker-compose up -d --build
   ```

Confluent Kafka comes with many containers. After waiting about 10 minutes for the containers to finish launching, go to a browser and navigate to `localhost:9091` to see Kafka Control Center.

How it works...

Kafka uses a journal to record data coming from end users into topics. These topics can then be read by consumers of the data. What has made Kafka a popular tool among the IoT community is its advanced features. Multiple streams can be combined, and streams can be turned into a key/value-based table where the most recent stream updates the table. But most importantly for the purpose of this book, ML algorithms can be run on streaming data with latency times in milliseconds. This recipe shows how to push data into Kafka and then create a Java project to manipulate the data in real time.

There's more...

Streaming data into Kafka is fairly easy. There are producers that send device-to-cloud messages and consumers that receive cloud-to-device messages. In the following example, we are going to implement a producer:

1. Download an example project:

    ```
    git clone https://github.com/Microshak/KafkaWeatherStreamer.git
    cd KafkaWeatherStreamer
    ```

2. Install the requirements:

    ```
    pip install -r requirements.txt
    ```

3. Run the `weather.py` file:

    ```
    python3 weather.py
    ```

You should now be able to look at your Kafka Control Center and see data flowing in. The Kafka Streams API is a real-time platform that can perform ML computations with millisecond latency. The Streams API has the concepts of KTables and KStreams. KStreams are data streaming into Kafka on various topics. KTables are streams turned into tables where the data is updated every time there is a new record associated with its primary key. This allows multiple streams to be joined together similarly to how tables in a database are joined together, giving Kafka the ability to not only deal with a single device at a time but also to take device data from multiple sources where we combine streams together.

To use the Streams API, you must first install Java and Maven on your computer. In addition, you will need to install an **integrated development environment** (IDE) for developing in Java, such as IntelliJ. Once you have installed all the prerequisites, run the Maven archetype to generate the code needed to start a Kafka Streams API project:

```
mvn archetype:generate \
    -DarchetypeGroupId=org.apache.kafka \
    -DarchetypeArtifactId=streams-quickstart-java \
    -DarchetypeVersion=2.2.0 \
    -DgroupId=streams.examples \
    -DartifactId=streams.examples \
    -Dversion=0.1 \
    -Dpackage=myapps
```

Open the newly created project in IntelliJ and you will be all set to code against the Kafka Streams API. The motto of Confluent, the maker of Kafka, is: *It's just Java*. What they mean by that is once you are in the Streams API, you can write Java code to do whatever you want. This could be to send out WebSocket information to a website or to run ML models. If it can be done in Java, then you can do it in the KStreams event loop. There are frameworks such as `deeplearning4j` that can take Keras models trained in Python and run them in Java.

Installing ML libraries on Databricks

Databricks is a unified big data and analytics platform. It is great for training ML models and working with the kind of large-scale data that is often found in IoT. There are extensions such as Delta Lake that allow researchers the ability to view data as it existed at certain periods of time so that they can do analysis when models drift. There are also tools such as MLflow that allow the data scientist to compare multiple models against each other. In this recipe, we are going to install various ML packages such as TensorFlow, PyTorch, and GraphFrames on Databricks. Most ML packages can be installed via PyPI. The format used to install TensorFlow, for example, will work on various ML frameworks such as OpenAI Gym, Sonnet, Keras, and MXNet. Some tools are available in Databricks that are not available in Python. For those, we use the pattern explored by GraphX and GraphFrame where packages are installed through Java extensions.

Getting ready

Before we start, it's important to know how the components work with each other. Let's start with workspaces. The workspace area is where you can share results between data scientists and engineers through the use of Databricks notebooks. Notebooks can interoperate with the filesystem in Databricks to store Parquet or Delta Lake files. The workspaces section also stores files such as Python libraries and JAR files. In the workspaces section, you can create folders to store shared files. I typically create a `packages` folder to store the Python and JAR files. Before we install the Python packages, let's first examine what a cluster is by going to the cluster section.

In your Databricks instance, go to the **Clusters** menu. You can create a cluster or use a cluster that has already been created. With clusters, you specify the amount of compute needed. Spark can work over large datasets but also work with GPUs for ML-optimized workloads. Some clusters have ML tools such as Conda preinstalled and others allow you to install your own libraries.

How to do it...

Traditional ML notebooks can have issues with different versions of ML packages installed. Databricks circumvents this by allowing users to set up resources that have a set of preinstalled packages. In this recipe, we're going to install various ML packages into Databricks. These packages can then be assigned to all new clusters going forward or specific clusters. This gives data scientists the flexibility to work with new versions of ML packages but still support older ML models they have developed. We will look at this recipe in three parts.

Importing TensorFlow

Perhaps the easiest way to import a Python library such as TensorFlow is to use PyPI. Simply go to `https://pypi.org/` and search for TensorFlow. This will give you the information needed and the ability to look at different versions. The installation steps are as follows:

1. Go to `https://pypi.org/` and search for TensorFlow.
2. Copy the name and version number you want in this format: `tensorflow==1.14.0`.
3. In the **Workspace** tab of Databricks, right-click anywhere and from the dropdown, click on **Create** and then **Library**:

4. On the **Create Library** page, select **PyPI** as the library source:

5. Copy the name of the library and the version number and paste that into the **Package** section.
6. Click **Create**.

If you have already created a cluster, you can attach TensorFlow to it. You can also have TensorFlow installed on all clusters.

Installing PyTorch

PyTorch is a popular ML library written in native Python and has built-in support for GPUs. Installing PyTorch is very similar to installing TensorFlow. You can install it via PyPI in the **Create | Library** menu choice. In the PyPI import library menu, put in the current version of PyPI (`torch==1.1.0.post2`). The installation steps are as follows:

1. Go to `https://pypi.org/` and search for PyTorch.
2. Copy the name and version number you want in this format: `torch==1.1.0.post2`.
3. In the **Workspace** tab of Databricks, right-click anywhere and from the dropdown, click on **Create** and then **Library**.

4. Select **PyPI** as the library source.
5. Copy the name of the library and the version number and paste that into the **Package** section.
6. Click **Create**.

If you have already created a cluster, you can attach PyTorch to it. You can also install PyTorch on all clusters.

Installing GraphX and GraphFrames

Spark has some distributed libraries that are not available anywhere else in data science. GraphFrames is one of them. In graph theory, you can perform actions such as finding the shortest path, network flow, homophily, centrality, and influence. Because GraphFrames is built on GraphX, which is a Java library, you need to install the Java library, and then to use the Python wrapper, you will need to `pip` install the Python library that accesses the Java JAR file. The installation steps are as follows:

1. Download a JAR file from `https://spark-packages.org/package/graphframes/graphframes`. You'll need to find a version that matches the version of Spark that you are running in your cluster.
2. In the **Workspace** tab of Databricks, right-click anywhere and from the dropdown, click on **Create** and then **Library**.
3. Drag and drop the JAR file into the space titled **Drop JAR here**.
4. Click **Create**.
5. Then, import another library.
6. In the **Workspace** tab of Databricks, right-click anywhere and from the dropdown, click on **Create** and then **Library**.
7. Select **PyPI** as the library source and enter `graphframes` in the **Package** section.
8. Click **Create**.

To test your installation, you can download a sample notebook and data files here: `https://github.com/Microshak/Databricks/tree/master/Graph`.

How it works...

Being designed for both data engineers and data scientists, Databricks supports multi-versions of software and multi-languages. It does this by allowing the installation of different versions of ML packages by allowing the user to configure each cluster separately. TensorFlow is installed implicitly on the streaming cluster. Another cluster has the popular Conda environment installed. Finally, the test environment does not have TensorFlow installed.

2
Handling Data

The technique used to collect data often determines the type of models that can be utilized. If a seismograph only reported the current reading of seismic activity once an hour, it would be meaningless. The data would not be high fidelity enough to predict earthquakes. The job of a data scientist in an IoT project does not start after the data is collected but rather, the data scientist needs to be part of the building of the device. When a device is built, the data scientist needs to determine whether the device is emitting the type of data that is appropriate for machine learning. Next, the data scientist helps the electrical engineer determine whether the sensors are in the right places and whether there is a correlation between sensors, and finally, the data scientist needs to store data in a way that is efficient to perform analytics. By doing so, we avoid the first major pitfall of IoT, which is collecting and storing data that is, in the end, useless for machine learning.

This chapter examines storing, collecting, and analyzing data to ensure that there is enough data to perform effective and efficient machine learning. We are going to start by looking at how data is stored and accessed. Then, we are going to look at data collection design to ensure that the data coming off the device is feasible for machine learning.

This chapter will cover the following recipes:

- Storing data for analysis using Delta Lake
- Data collection design
- Windowing
- Exploratory factor analysis
- Implementing analytic queries in Mongo/hot path storage
- Ingesting IoT data into Spark

Storing data for analysis using Delta Lake

Today, there are many options for dealing with data for analysis. You can store it in a data lake, Delta Lake, or a NoSQL database. This recipe covers data storage and retrieval and using Delta Lake. Delta Lake provides the fastest way to work with data and the most efficient way to store data. It also allows you to look at data as it existed at any given time in the past.

Getting ready

While Delta Lake is an open source project, the easiest way to store files in Delta Lake is through Databricks. The setup of Databricks was discussed in Chapter 1, *Setting Up the IoT and AI Environment*. This recipe assumes you have Databricks set up and running.

How to do it...

Importing files into Delta Lake is easy. Data can be imported through files or streaming. The steps for this recipe are as follows:

1. In Databricks, open the data panel by clicking on the **Data** button, click on the **Add Data** button, and drag your file into the **Upload** section.
2. Click on **Create Table in Notebook**. The code generated for you will start with this:

```
# File location and type
file_location = "/FileStore/tables/soilmoisture_dataset.csv"
file_type = "csv"

# CSV options
infer_schema = "false"
```

```
first_row_is_header = "false"
delimiter = ","

df = spark.read.format(file_type) \
  .option("inferSchema", infer_schema) \
  .option("header", first_row_is_header) \
  .option("sep", delimiter) \
  .load(file_location)

display(df)
```

3. Review the data and when you are ready to save to Delta Lake, uncomment the last line:

```
# df.write.format("parquet").saveAsTable(permanent_table_name)
```

4. Then, change "`parquet`" to "`delta`":

```
df.write.format("delta").saveAsTable(permanent_table_name)
```

5. From here, query the data:

```
%sql
SELECT * FROM soilmoisture
```

6. Alternatively, you can optimize how Delta Lake saves the file, making querying faster:

```
%sql
OPTIMIZE soilmoisture ZORDER BY (deviceid)
```

Delta Lake data can be updated, filtered, and aggregated. In addition, it can be turned into a Spark or Koalas DataFrame easily.

How it works...

Delta Lake is built on top of Parquet. Utilizing columnar compression and metadata storage, it can make the retrieval of data 10 times faster than standard Parquet. In addition to faster performance, Delta Lake's data versioning allows data scientists to look at how data was at a particular time, allowing data scientists to perform root cause analysis when their models drift.

Data collection design

The single most important factor in machine learning and IoT is data collection design. If the data collected is *garbage data*, then no machine learning can be done on top of it. Suppose you are looking at vibrations of a pump (shown in the following graph) to determine whether the pump is having issues with its mechanics or ball bearings so that preventive maintenance can be performed before serious damage is done to the machine:

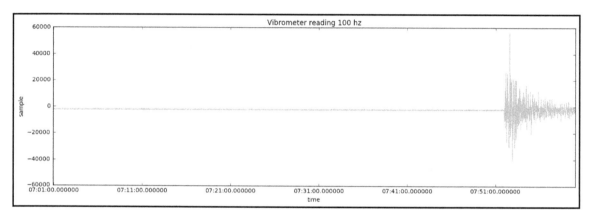

Importantly, real-time data at 100 Hz is prohibitively expensive to store in the cloud. To keep costs down, engineers often send data at frequencies of 1 minute. Low-frequency sensor data often cannot accurately represent the issue that is being looked at. The next chart shows how the data looks when only sampled once per minute:

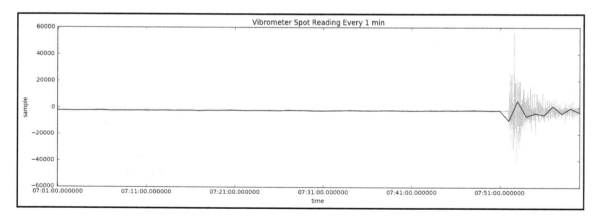

Here, we see vibrometer data overlaid with the data that is being collected in 1-minute intervals. The data has some use but it is not accurate as it does not show the true magnitude of what is going on with the data. Using the mean is worse. The following chart shows the average reading of the vibrometer's mean over 1 minute:

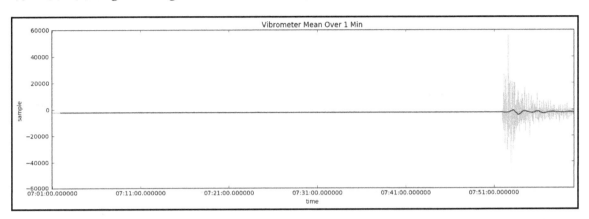

Taking the average reading windowed over 1 minute is an even worse solution because the average value is not changing when there is a problem with the pump. The following chart shows the vibrometer's standard reading over 1 minute:

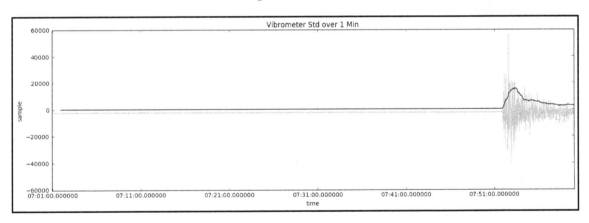

Using a standard deviation technique shows variance compared to the mean to determine whether there is an issue with the pump. This is a more accurate solution over the average technique.

Using minimum and maximum windowed over a 1-minute window can present the best representation of the magnitude of the situation. The following chart shows what the reading will look like:

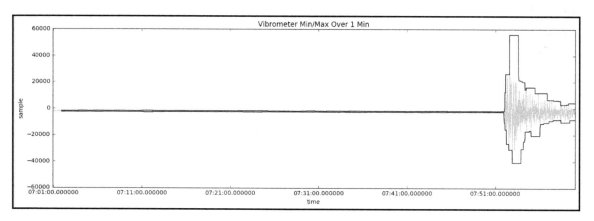

Because IoT machines can work correctly for years before having issues and forwarding high-frequency data in the cloud is cost-prohibitive, other measurements are used to determine whether the device needs maintenance. Techniques such as *min/max, standard deviation*, or *spikes* can be used to trigger a cloud-to-device message telling the device to send data at a much higher frequency. High-frequency diagnostic data can use blob storage to store large files.

One of the challenges of IoT is finding meaningful data in a sea of data. In this recipe, we shall demonstrate techniques to mine for valuable data.

Getting ready

To get ready for data collection design, you will need a device streaming data at a high rate. In Chapter 1, *Setting Up the IoT and AI Environment*, we discussed getting a device streaming data into IoT Hub. Often in production, device data is sent in intervals of 15 seconds or 1 minute. But for data collection design, one device is sending data at a high rate of 10 Hz, or 10 times a second. Once that data is flowing in, you can pull it into Databricks for real-time analysis.

How to do it...

In our Databricks notebooks, we will analyze of the IoT data using techniques such as variance, Z-Spikes, and min/max.

Variance

Variance is the measure of how much the data varies from the mean. In the code that follows, we are using Koalas, a distributed clone of `pandas`, to do our basic data engineering tasks, such as determining variance. The following code uses standard deviation over a rolling window to show data spike issues:

```
import databricks.koalas as ks

df = ks.DataFrame(pump_data)
print("variance: " + str(df.var()))
minuite['time'] = pd.to_datetime(minuite['time'])
minuite.set_index('time')
minuite['sample'] =
minuite['sample'].rolling(window=600,center=False).std()
```

Duty cycles are used on IoT product lines before enough data is collected for machine learning. They are often simple measures, such as whether the device is too hot or there are too many vibrations.

We can also look at high and low values such as maximum to show whether the sensor is throwing out appropriate readings. The following code shows the maximum reading of our dataset:

```
max = DF.agg({"averageRating": "max"}).collect()[0]
```

Z-Spikes

Spikes can help determine whether there is an issue by looking at how rapidly a reading is changing. For example, an outdoor IoT device may have a different operating temperature in the South Pole compared to one in direct sun in Death Valley. One way of finding out whether there is an issue with the device is by looking at how fast the temperature is changing. Z-Spikes are a typical time-based anomaly detection. It is used because it only looks at that device's readings and can give a value independent of environmental factors.

Z-Spikes look at how the spike differs from the standard deviation. They use a statistical z-test to determine whether a spike is greater than 99.5% of the population.

Min/max

Mins and maxes can show the value that shows the most stress on the system. The following code shows how to get the min and max values of a 1-minute window:

```
minute['max'] = minute['sample'].rolling(window=600,center=False).max()

minute['sample'] = minute['sample'].rolling(window=600,center=False).min()
```

Minimum and maximum values can emphasize outliers. This can be useful in determining anomalies.

Windowing

There are three primary windowing functions: tumbling, hopping, and sliding. Both Spark and Stream Analytics can do windowing. Windowing allows you to look at aggregate functions such as average, count, and sum. It also allows you to look at minimum and maximum values. Windowing is a feature engineering technique to help make data more manageable. In this recipe, we are going to cover several tools for windowing and the ways to window.

Getting ready

To get ready, you will also need a device streaming data to IoT Hub. That stream will need to be ingested by either Azure's Stream Analytics, Spark, or Databricks.

How to do it...

Utilize a Databricks notebook or Stream Analytics workspace to perform the recipes. Windowing turns the static of large datasets into meaningful features of your machine learning model.

Tumbling

Tumbling window functions group data streams into time segments (as shown in the following diagram). Tumbling windows means that the window does not repeat or overlap data from one segment waterfall into the next:

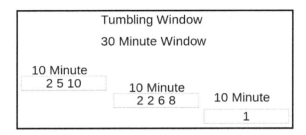

Stream Analytics

In Stream Analytics, one way to use a tumbling window to count the events that happen every 10 seconds would be to do the following:

```
SELECT EventTime, Count(*) AS Count
FROM DeviceStream TIMESTAMP BY CreatedAt
GROUP by EventTime, TumbelingWindow(minuites, 10)
```

Spark

In Spark, to do the same count of events happening every 10 minutes, you would do the following:

```
from pyspark.sql.functions import *
windowedDF = eventsDF.groupBy(window("eventTime", "10 minute")).count()
```

Hopping

Hopping windows are tumbling windows that overlap. They allow you to set specific commands and conditions, such as *every 5 minutes, give me the count of the sensor readings over the last 10 minutes*. To make a hopping window the same as a tumbling window, you would make the hop size the same as the window size, as shown in the following diagram:

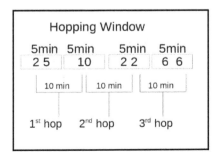

Stream Analytics

The following Stream Analytics example shows a count of messages over a 10-minute window. This count happens every 5 minutes:

```
SELECT EventTime, Count(*) AS Count
FROM DeviceStream TIMESTAMP BY CreatedAt
GROUP by EventTime, HopingWindow(minuites, 10, 5)
```

Spark

In PySpark, this would be done through a window function. The following example shows a Spark DataFrame that is windowed, producing an entry in a new entry in a DataFrame for every 5 minutes spanning a 10-minute period:

```
from pyspark.sql.functions import *
windowedDF = eventsDF.groupBy(window("eventTime", "10 minute", "5
minute")).count()
```

Sliding

Sliding windows produce an output when an event occurs. The following diagram illustrates this concept:

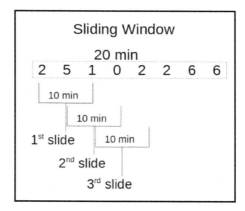

Stream Analytics

In the Stream Analytics example, by using a sliding window, we only receive a result when there are more than 100 messages over a 10-minute window. Unlike other methods that look at an exact window of time and show one message for that window, in sliding windows, we would receive a message on every input message. Another use of this would be to show a rolling average:

```
SELECT EventTime, Count(*) AS Count
FROM DeviceStream TIMESTAMP BY CreatedAt
GROUP by EventTime,
SlidingWindow(minutes, 10)
WHERE COUNT(*) > 100
```

How it works...

Using windowing, IoT data can show factors such as frequency, sums, standard deviation, and percentile distribution over a period of time. Windowing can be used to enrich the data with feature engineering or can transform the data into an aggregate dataset. Windowing, for example, can show how many devices were produced in a factory or show the modulation in a sensor reading.

Exploratory factor analysis

Garbage data is one of the key issues that plague IoT. Data is often not validated before it is collected. Often, there are issues with bad sensor placement or data that appears to be random because it is not an appropriate measure for the type of data being used. For example, a vibrometer may show, because of the central limit theorem, that the data is centered around the mean, whereas the data is actually showing a large increase in magnitude. To combat this, it is important to do exploratory factor analysis on the device data.

In this recipe, we will explore several techniques of factor analysis. Aggregate data and raw telemetry data are used in Databricks notebooks to perform this analysis.

Getting ready

You will need to have data in a table in Databricks, which we implemented in the *Storing data for analysis using Delta Lake* recipe. Once data is in a Spark data table, it is ready for factor analysis.

How to do it...

This recipe is composed of two sections. The first is performing a visual inspection of data. Visual inspection can reveal software bugs, learn about how the device behaves, and determine device data patterns. The second part looks at correlation and co-variance. These techniques are often used to determine whether a sensor is redundant.

Visual exploration

Spark allows you to look at basic charts without much code. Using the magic symbol at the top of the notebook segment, you can change language easily from Python to Scala or SQL. One word of caution about using Databricks' built-in charting system is that it only looks at the first 10,000 records. For a large dataset, there are other charting libraries. The steps are as follows:

1. Query the data in Databricks using the `%sql` magic, as shown:

```
%sql
select * from Telemetry
```

2. Select the chart icon at the bottom of the returned data grid. It will bring up the chart builder UI, as shown in the following screenshot:

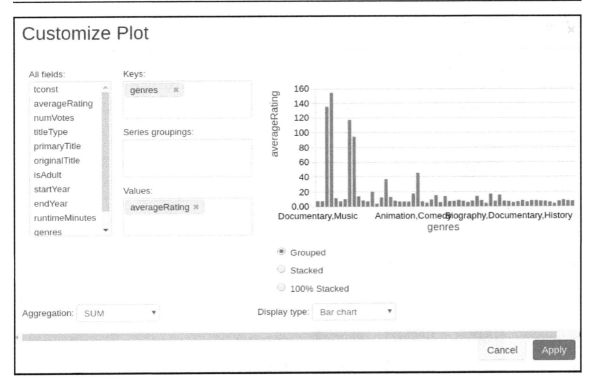

3. Select the chart type that best represents the data. Some charts are better suited for variable comparison while others can help reveal trends.

The following section reviews when and why you would use different chart types.

Chart types

Different types of charts illuminate different aspects of the data, such as comparison, composition, relationship, and distribution. Relationship charts are used to test a hypothesis or look at how one factor affects other factors. Composition shows the percentage breakdown of a dataset. It is often used to show how factors compare against others. A pie chart is a simple composition chart. Distribution charts are used to show distributions of a population. They are often used to determine whether the data is random, has a large spread, or is normalized. Comparison charts are used to compare one value against others.

Bar and column charts

Bar and column charts are used to make a comparison between items. Bar charts can have many items simply because of the page layout. Column and bar charts can also show change over time. The following chart is an example of a bar and column chart:

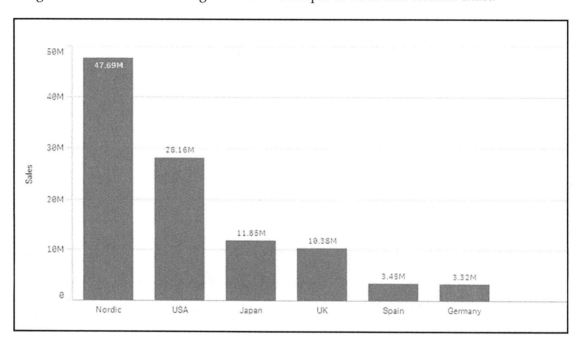

Scatter plot

Scatter plots can show the relationship between two variables. It also can show a trend line. The following is an example of a scatter plot:

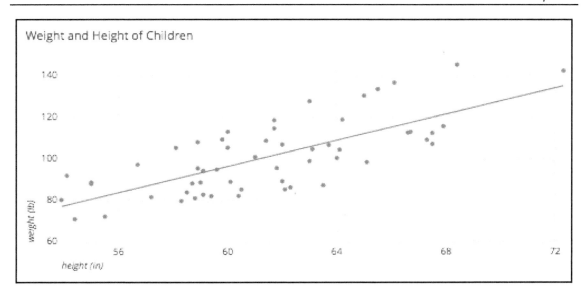

Bubble charts

When you want to show the relationship between three variables, you can use bubble charts. This can be used to show anomalous behavior. The following is an example of a bubble chart:

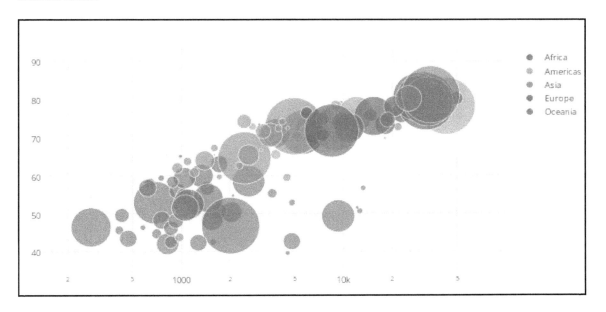

Line charts

These charts show changes over time and can be used to show how a device's data changes over a day. If a device has seasonal data, you may need to include the time of day as part of the algorithm or use de-seasonal algorithms. The following is an example of a line chart:

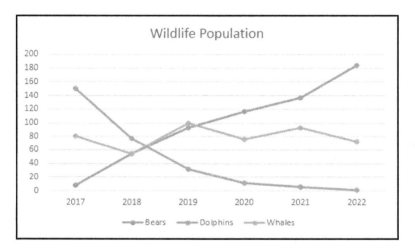

Area charts

Area charts are like line charts but are used to show how the volume of one segment compares to another. The following is an example of an area chart:

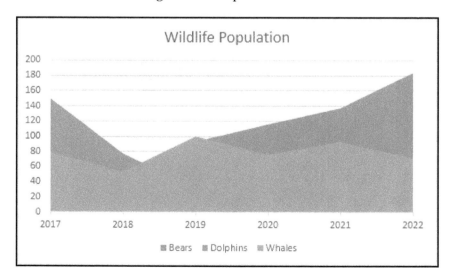

Quantile plot

Help determine population shape by spitting data into segments (quantiles). Common quantiles are 25%, 50%, and 75%, or 33% and 66%, or 5% and 95% (percentages in general are quartiles). Understanding whether data is behaving within expected parameters is important in understanding whether a device is having problems. The following is an example of a quantile plot:

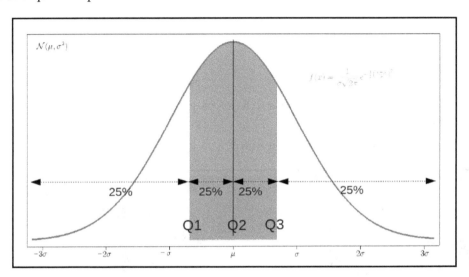

Redundant sensors

One of the challenges of IoT is determining where to place the sensors and how many sensors are needed. Take pumps, for example: one way of determining whether a pump's bearings are going out is to use a microphone to listen for a high-pitched squeal. Another way is to use a parameter to determine whether it is vibrating more. Yet another way is to measure the current and see whether it is fluctuating. There is no one right way to determine whether a pump's ball bearings are going out; however, implementing all three techniques may be cost-prohibitive and redundant. A common way of looking at the correlation between different sensors is using a heat map. In the following code, we use a heat map to find the correlation between sensors. In other words, we are looking for sensors that are transmitting redundant information:

```
import numpy as np
import pandas as pd
import matplotlib.pyplot as plt
import seaborn as sns
```

```
# load the sample training data
train = pd.read_csv('/dbfs/FileStore/tables/Bike_train.csv')

for i in range(50):
    a = np.random.normal(5,i+1,10)
    b.append(a)
c = np.array(b)
cm =np.corrcoef(c)

plt.imshow(cm,interpolation='nearest')
plt.colorbar()

#heat map
plt.figure(figsize=(17,11))
sns.heatmap(train.iloc[:,1:30].corr(), cmap= 'viridis', annot=True)
display(plt.show())
```

The following screenshot shows the heat map:

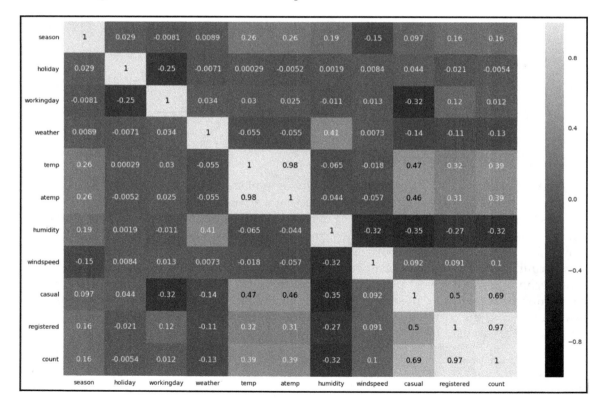

In the preceding example, we can see that `count` and `registered` have a very high correlation because both numbers are close to 1. Similarly, we can see that `temp` and `atemp` have a high degree of correlation. Using this data without pruning out the corollary data can give a weighted effect to machine learning models training on the dataset.

 When a device has very little data, it still may be valuable to perform analysis of variance, distribution, and deviation. Because it has a lower bar of entry than machine learning, it can be deployed at an earlier phase in the machine's life cycle. Doing statistical analysis helps ensure that the device is setting proper data that is not duplicated or false and can be used for machine learning.

Cross-tabulation provides a table of the frequency distributions. This can be used to determine whether two different sensors are counting the same. The following is the code to display the cross-tabulation table:

```
display(DF.stat.crosstab("titleType", "genres"))
```

Sample co-variance and correlation

Co-variance measures the joint variability change of two sensors with respect to each other. Positive numbers would indicate that the sensors are reporting the same data. Negative numbers indicate that there is an inverse relationship between the sensors. The co-variance of two sensors can be calculated using the DataFrame `stat.cov` function in a Spark DataFrame:

```
df.stat.cov('averageRating', 'numVotes')
```

How it works...

Modifying physical devices after they have been produced can be costly. This recipe shows how to inspect a prototype device to make sure the data produced by it will not be meaningless. Using data analysis tools such as Databricks for preliminary data analysis can save us from issues that plague IoT and AI, such as bad sensor placement, under- or overcommunication, and data that is not usable for machine learning. Performing standard machine learning tasks such as predictive maintenance, anomaly detection, or remaining useful life is dependent on good data.

There's more...

You can further explore data by creating a filtering widget. For example, you could use the `CREATE WIDGET DROPDOWN` query as shown:

```
%sql
CREATE WIDGET DROPDOWN tytleType DEFAULT "movie" CHOICES SELECT DISTINCT
titleType FROM imdbTitles
```

Creating a widget allows you to create a data query that can be easily segmented, as shown in the following code:

```
%sql
select * from imdbTitles where titleType = getArgument("tytleType")
```

Other widget types, such as text, combo box, and multi-select, also are available.

Implementing analytic queries in Mongo/hot path storage

In IoT architectures, there is hot and cold path data. Hot path data can be accessed immediately. This is typically stored in a NoSQL or time-series database. An example of this would be to use a time-series database such as InfluxDB to count the number of resets per device over the last hour. This could be used to aid in feature engineering. Another use of hot data is precision analysis. If a machine breaks in the field, a database such as MongoDB can be queried for just the data that that machine has generated over the last month.

Cold path data is typically used for batch processing, such as machine learning and monthly reports. Cold path data is primarily data stored in a blob, S3 storage, or HDFS-compliant data store. Separating a hot path from a cold path is usually a factor of cost and scalability. IoT data generally falls into the category of big data. If a data scientist queries years' worth of data from a NoSQL database, the web application that is using it can falter. The same is not true for data stored in the cold path on a disk. On the other hand, if the data scientist needs to query a few hundred records from billions of records, a NoSQL database would be appropriate.

This recipe is focused on working with hot data. This recipe's primary focus is on extracting IoT data from MongoDB. First, we extract data from one device, and then we will aggregate it across multiple devices.

Getting ready

Stream Analytics can get IoT data into MongoDB. To do this, start up MongoDB. This can be done through Azure Kubernetes Service or using the Atlas MongoDB cloud provider. Once you have a database, you can use a function app to move data between IoT Hub and MongoDB.

How to do it...

Mongo has a list of filtering options comparable to SQL. The following code shows how to connect to a local version of Mongo and query for all products with an inventory status of A:

```
df = spark.read.format("mongo").option("uri",
"mongodb://127.0.0.1/products.inventory").load()
pipeline =  "{'deviceid':'8ea23889-3677-4ebe-80b6-3fee6e38a42c'}"
df = spark.read.format("mongo").option("pipeline", pipeline).load()
df.show()
```

The next example shows how to do a complicated filter followed by a group by operation. It finally sums the information. The output will show the count of items with a status of A:

```
pipeline = "[ { '$match': { 'status': 'A' } }, { '$group': { '_id':
'$item', 'total': { '$sum': '$qty' } } } ]"
df = spark.read.format("mongo").option("pipeline", pipeline).load()
df.show()
```

How it works...

Mongo stores indexed data on multiple computers or partitions. This allows retrieval of specific data to be done with latency times in milliseconds. NoSQL databases can provide fast lookup for data. In this recipe, we discussed how to query data from MongoDB into Databricks.

Ingesting IoT data into Spark

To connect Spark to IoT Hub, first, create a consumer group. A consumer group is a pointer to the current position in the journal that the consumer has reached. There can be multiple consumers on the same journal of data. The consumer group is paralyzed and distributable, enabling you to write programs that can remain stable even on a massive scale.

Getting ready

For this recipe, go into the Azure IoT Hub portal and click on the **Build-in endpoints** menu option. Then, add a consumer group by entering some text. While still on that screen, copy the **Event Hub-compatible endpoint** connection string.

How to do it...

The steps for this recipe are as follows:

1. In Databricks, start a new notebook and enter the information needed to connect to IoT Hub. Then, enter the following code:

```
import datetime as dt
import json

ehConf = {}
ehConf['eventhubs.connectionString'] = ["The connection string you
copies"]
ehConf['eventhubs.consumerGroup'] = "[The consumer group you
created]"

startingEventPosition = {
  "offset": -1,
  "seqNo": -1, #not in use
  "enqueuedTime": None, #not in use
  "isInclusive": True
}

endingEventPosition = {
  "offset": None, #not in use
  "seqNo": -1, #not in use
  "enqueuedTime": endTime,
  "isInclusive": True
}
ehConf["eventhubs.recieverTimeout"] = 100
```

2. Put the data into a Spark DataFrame:

```
df = spark \
 .readStream \
 .format("eventhubs") \
 .options(**ehConf) \
 .load()
```

3. The next step is to apply a structure to the data so that you can use structured streaming:

```
from pyspark.sql.types import *
Schema = StructType([StructField("deviceEndSessionTime",
StringType()), StructField("sensor1", StringType()),
 StructField("sensor2", StringType()),
 StructField("deviceId", LongType()),
 ])
```

4. The final step is to apply the schema to a DataFrame. This allows you to work with the data as if it were a table:

```
from pyspark.sql.functions import *

rawData = df. \
  selectExpr("cast(Body as string) as json"). \
  select(from_json("json", Schema).alias("data")). \
 select("data.*")
```

How it works...

In this recipe, we connected to IoT Hub and put the data into a DataFrame. Later, we added a structure to that frame, allowing us to query data similarly to the way we query a database table.

In the next few chapters, we will discuss how to create models. After creating models using cold path data, you can perform near-real-time machine learning on it by pushing those trained models into Databricks structured streaming.

Machine Learning for IoT 3

Machine learning has dramatically altered what manufacturers are able to do with IoT. Today, there are numerous industries that have specific IoT needs. For example, the **internet of medical things (IoMT)** has devices such as outpatient heart monitors that can be worn at home. These devices often require large amounts of data to be sent over the network or large compute capacity on the edge to process heart-related events. Another example is **agricultural IoT (AIoT)** devices that are often placed in locations where there is no Wi-Fi or cellular network. Prescriptions or models are pushed down to these semi-connected devices. Many of these devices require that decisions be made on the edge. When connectivity is finally established using technology such as LoRAWAN or TV, white space models are downloaded to the devices.

In this chapter, we are going to discuss using machine learning models such as logistic regression and decision trees to solve common IoT issues such as classifying medical results, detecting unsafe drivers, and classifying chemical readings. We are also going to look at techniques for working with constrained devices, and we are going to look at using unsupervised learning to gain insights on devices with little data, such as prototypes.

This chapter contains the following recipes:

- Analyzing chemical sensors with anomaly detection
- Logistic regression with IoMT
- Classifying chemical sensors with decision trees
- Simple predictive maintenance with XGBoost
- Detecting unsafe drivers
- Face detection on constrained devices

Analyzing chemical sensors with anomaly detection

Accurate predictive models require a large number of devices in the field to have failed so that they have enough fail data to use for predictions. For some well-crafted industrial devices, failures on this scale can take years. Anomaly detection can identify devices that are not behaving like the other devices in the fleet. It can also be used to wade through thousands of similar messages and pinpoint the messages that are not like the others.

Anomaly detection in machine learning can be **unsupervised, supervised,** or **semi-supervised**. Usually, it starts by using an unsupervised machine learning algorithm to cluster data into patterns of behavior or groups. This presents a series of data in buckets. When the machines are examined, some of the buckets identify behavior while some identify an issue with the device. The device may have exhibited different patterns of behavior in a resting state, an in-use state, a cold state, or something that represents a state that needs to be investigated.

This recipe presumes the use of a dataset where not much is known about the data. The process of anomaly detection is used as part of the discovery process and is often used with prototypes.

Getting ready

Anomaly detection is one of the easiest machine learning models to implement. In this recipe, we are going to use a dataset drawn from chemical sensors that are detecting either neutral, banana, or wine. To get ready, you will need to import the `numpy`, `sklearn` and `matplotlib` libraries.

How to do it...

The following steps need to be observed to complete this recipe:

1. Import the required libraries:

   ```
   import numpy as np
   from sklearn.cluster import KMeans
   import matplotlib.pyplot as plt
   ```

2. Upload the data file to a DataFrame:

```
df = spark.read.format("csv" \
    .option("inferSchema", True) \
    .option("header", True) \
    .option("sep", "\t") \
    .load("/FileStore/tables/HT_Sensor_metadata.dat")
```

3. View the dataset to see if the grouping of data correlates to the number of clusters:

```
pdf = df.toPandas()

y_pred = KMeans(n_clusters=3,
                random_state=2).fit_predict(pdf[['dt','t0']])


plt.scatter(pdf['t0'],pdf['dt'], c=y_pred)
display(plt.show())
```

The output is as follows:

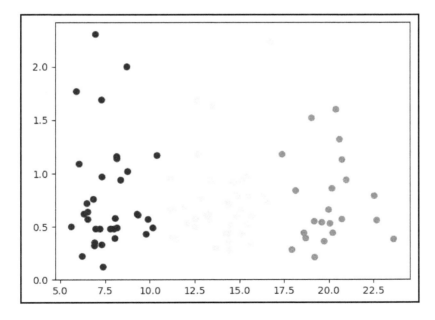

The preceding chart shows three different groups of data. Tight clusters represent data with well-defined boundaries. If we adjust the number of clusters to 10, we may be able to get better separation of different groups. These cluster segments help us identify different segments of data. This, in turn, may help us determine optimal sensor placement for a prototype or perform feature engineering in a machine learning model.

How it works...

In this recipe, we are using `numpy` for data manipulation, `sklearn` for the machine learning algorithm, and `matplotlib` for viewing the results. Next, we pull the tab-separated file into a Spark dataframe. In this step, we convert the data into a pandas DataFrame. Then we run the k-means algorithm with three clusters, which gives the chart as the output.

K-means is an algorithm that helps group data into clusters. K-means is a popular clustering algorithm for examining data without labels. K-means first randomly initializes cluster centroids. In our example, it had three cluster centroids. It then assigns the centroids to the nearest data points. Next, it moves each centroid to the spot that is in the middle of its respective cluster. It repeats these steps until it achieves an appropriate division of data points.

There's more...

In the chart, you may have noticed outliers. These are very important to note when looking at prototypes. Outliers can represent power fluctuations within a machine, bad sensor placement, or a number of other issues. The following example shows a simple standard deviation calculation on our data. From here, we are able to see two values that fall outside three standard deviations from the mean:

```
from numpy import mean
from numpy import std

data_mean, data_std = mean(pdf['dt']), std(pdf['dt'])

cut_off = data_std * 3
lower, upper = data_mean - cut_off, data_mean + cut_off

outliers = [x for x in pdf['dt'] if x < lower or x > upper]
print('Identified outliers: %d' % len(outliers))
print(outliers)
```

Logistic regression with the IoMT

In this recipe, we're going to talk about using logistic regression to classify data from mammography machines. Recently, the IoMT has expanded greatly. Many devices are being worn by patients when they go home from their doctor, providing an in-home medical monitoring solution, while others are in hospitals, giving the doctors additional feedback on medical tests being run. In many cases, machine learning algorithms are able to spot diseases and issues that doctors may miss, or give them additional recommendations. In this recipe, we are going to work with a breast cancer dataset and determine whether a mammogram record is malignant or benign.

Getting ready

The dataset, along with the Databricks notebooks, is available in the GitHub repository. The dataset is unwieldy. It has bad columns with a high degree of correlation, which is another way of saying some sensors are duplicates, and there are unused columns and extraneous data. For the sake of readability, there will be two notebooks in the GitHub repository. The first does all of the data manipulation and puts the data into a data table. The second notebook does the machine learning. We will focus this recipe on the data manipulation notebook. At the end of the recipe, we will talk about two other notebooks to show an example of MLflow.

One other thing you will need in this recipe is an MLflow workspace. To set up an MLflow workspace, you will need to go into Databricks and create the workspace for this experiment. We will write the results of our experiment there.

How to do it...

Follow these steps to complete this recipe:

1. Import the required libraries:

```
import pandas as pd

from sklearn import neighbors, metrics
from sklearn.metrics import roc_auc_score, classification_report,\
precision_recall_fscore_support,confusion_matrix,precision_score, \
roc_curve,precision_recall_fscore_support as score
from sklearn.model_selection import train_test_split

import statsmodels.api as sm
import statsmodels.formula.api as smf
```

2. Import the data:

```
df = spark.sql("select * from BreastCancer")
pdf = df.toPandas()
```

3. Split the data:

```
X = pdf
y = pdf['diagnosis']

X_train, X_test, y_train, y_test = \
    train_test_split(X, y, test_size=0.3, random_state=40)
```

4. Create the formula:

```
cols = pdf.columns.drop('diagnosis')
formula = 'diagnosis ~ ' + ' + '.join(cols)
```

5. Train the model:

```
model = smf.glm(formula=formula, data=X_train,
                family=sm.families.Binomial())
logistic_fit = model.fit()
```

6. Test our model:

```
predictions = logistic_fit.predict(X_test)
predictions_nominal = [ "M" if x < 0.5 else "B" for x in \
                        predictions]
```

7. Evaluate the model:

```
print(classification_report(y_test, predictions_nominal, digits=3))
```

The output shows the `precision`, `recall`, and `f1-score` of malignant (M) and benign (B):

```
          precision    recall  f1-score

      B       0.957     0.957     0.957
      M       0.907     0.907     0.907
```

8. Evaluate the confusion matrix:

```
cfm = confusion_matrix(y_test, predictions_nominal)
precision,recall,fscore,support=score(y_test, predictions_nominal,
                                       average='macro')

print('Confusion Matrix: \n', cfm, '\n')
```

The output is as follows:

```
Confusion Matrix:
 [[112    5]
 [  5   49]]
```

The results show that out of 171 records in our testing set, 112 were true negatives and 49 were true positives, meaning that out of 171 records it was able to correctly identify 161 records. 10 of those predictions were wrong: 5 false negatives and 5 false positives.

How it works...

In this recipe, we used logistic regression. Logistic regression is a technique that can be used for traditional statistics as well as machine learning. Due to its simplicity and power, many data scientists use logistic regression as their first model and use it as a benchmark to beat. Logistic regression is a binary classifier, meaning it can classify something as `true` or `false`. In our case, the classifications are benign or malignant.

First, we import `koalas` for data manipulation and `sklearn` for our model and analysis. Next, we import data from our data table and put it into a Pandas DataFrame. Then we split the data into testing and training datasets. Next, we create a formula that will describe for the model the data columns being used. Next, we give the model the formula, the training dataset, and the algorithm it will use. We then output a model that we can use to evaluate new data. We now create a DataFrame called `predictions_nominal`, which we can use to compare against our testing results dataset. The classification report gives us `precision`, `recall`, and `f1-score`:

- **Precision**: The ratio of correctly reported positive predictions to the expected positive predictions
- **Recall**: The ratio of correctly reported positive predictions compared to the total population
- **F-score**: A blended score of precision and recall

Next, we can look at the results of the model and determine how accurately it predicted the real values. Some factors that we will examine are as follows:

- **True Negatives:** The predicted negatives that were actually negative in the test set
- **False Positives**: The number that the trained model predicted would be positive in the training set but were not
- **False Negatives**: The number of false negatives predicted in the test set that were actually positives
- **True Positives**: The amount the model actually got correct

There's more...

We will record the outcome in MLflow to be compared against other algorithms. We will also save other parameters, such as the main formula used and the family of predictions:

```
import pickle
import mlflow

with mlflow.start_run():
    mlflow.set_experiment("/Shared/experiments/BreastCancer")
    mlflow.log_param("formula", formula)
    mlflow.log_param("family", "binomial")
    mlflow.log_metric("precision", precision)
    mlflow.log_metric("recall", recall)
    mlflow.log_metric("fscore", fscore)
    filename = 'finalized_model.sav'
```

```
pickle.dump(model, open(filename, 'wb'))

mlflow.log_artifact(filename)
```

Classifying chemical sensors with decision trees

In this recipe, we are going to use chemical sensor data from **Metal-Oxide (MOx)** sensors to determine whether there is wine in the air. This type of sensor is commonly used to determine whether food or chemical particulates are in the air. Chemical sensors can detect gasses that would be poisonous to people or food spillage at a warehouse.

How to do it...

Follow these steps to complete this recipe:

1. Import the libraries:

```
import pandas as pd
import numpy as np

from sklearn import neighbors, metrics
from sklearn.model_selection import train_test_split
from sklearn.tree import DecisionTreeClassifier
from sklearn.preprocessing import OneHotEncoder
from sklearn.preprocessing import LabelEncoder
```

2. Import the data:

```
df = spark.sql("select * from ChemicalSensor")
pdf = df.toPandas()
```

3. Encode the values:

```
label_encoder = LabelEncoder()
integer_encoded = \
    label_encoder.fit_transform(pdf['classification'])
onehot_encoder = OneHotEncoder(sparse=False)

integer_encoded = integer_encoded.reshape(len(integer_encoded), 1)
onehot_encoded = onehot_encoder.fit_transform(integer_encoded)
```

4. Test/train the split data:

```
X = pdf[feature_cols]
y = onehot_encoded

X_train, X_test, y_train, y_test = \
train_test_split(X, y, test_size=0.2, random_state=5)
```

5. Train and predict:

```
clf = DecisionTreeClassifier()
clf = clf.fit(X_train,y_train)
y_pred = clf.predict(X_test)
```

6. Evaluate the accuracy:

```
print("Accuracy:",metrics.accuracy_score(y_test, y_pred))
print("AUC:",roc_auc_score(y_test, y_pred))
```

How it works...

As always, we import the libraries we need for this project. Next, we import data from our Spark data table into a Pandas DataFrame. One-hot encoding can change categorical values, such as our example of *Wine* and *No Wine*, into encoded values that machine learning algorithms can use better. In *step 4*, we take our feature columns and our one-hot encoded column and perform a split, splitting them into a testing and training set. In *step 5*, we create a decision tree classifier, use the X_train and y_train data to train the model, and then use the X_test data to create a y_prediction dataset. In other words, in the end, we will have a set of predictions called y_pred based on the predictions the dataset had on the X_test set. In *step 6*, we evaluate the accuracy of the model and the **area under the curve (AUC)**.

Decision tree classifiers are used when the data is complex. In the same way, you can use a decision tree to follow a set of logical rules using yes/no questions, as shown in the following diagram:

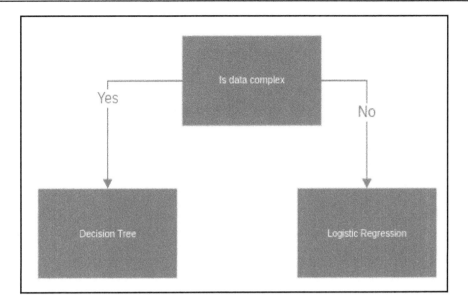

A machine learning algorithm can train a decision tree model to use numeric data, as shown in the following diagram:

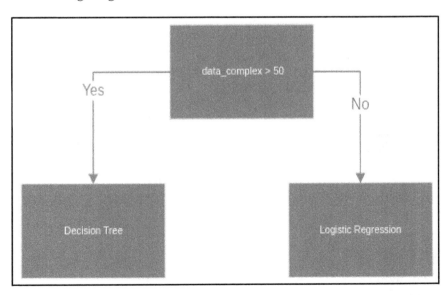

The machine learning algorithm trains the model to accurately pick the best path given the available data.

There's more...

The `sklearn` decision tree classifier has two hyperparameters that we can tune: **criterion** and **max depth**. Hyperparameters are often changed to see if accuracy can be increased. The criterion is either gini or entropy. Both of these criteria evaluate impurities in the child nodes. The next one is max depth. The max depth of the decision tree can affect over- and underfitting.

Underfitting versus overfitting
Models that underfit are inaccurate and poorly represent the data they were trained on.

Models that overfit are unable to generalize from the data trained on. It misses similar data to the training set because it only works on exactly the same data it was trained on.

Simple predictive maintenance with XGBoost

Every device has an end of life or will require maintenance from time to time. Predictive maintenance is one of the most commonly used machine learning algorithms in IoT. The next chapter will cover predictive maintenance in depth, looking at sequential data and how that data changes with seasonality. This recipe will look at predictive maintenance from the simpler perspective of classification.

In this recipe, we are going to use the NASA *Turbofan engine degradation simulation* dataset. We are going to be looking at having three classifications. Green means the engine does not need maintenance; yellow, the engine needs maintenance within the next 14 maintenance cycles; or red, the engine needs maintenance within the next cycle. For an algorithm, we are going to use **extreme gradient boosting** (**XGBoost**). XGBoost has become popular in recent years because it tends to win more Kaggle competitions than other algorithms.

Getting ready

To get ready you will need the NASA *Turbofan engine degradation simulation* dataset. The data, along with a Spark notebook, can be found in the companion GitHub repository for this book or on the NASA website. Next, you will need to make sure you install XGBoost as a library in Databricks.

How to do it...

The steps for this recipe are as follows:

1. Import the libraries:

```python
import pandas as pd
import numpy as np
from pyspark.sql.types import *
import xgboost as xgb
from sklearn.model_selection import train_test_split
from sklearn.metrics import precision_score
import pickle
import mlflow
```

2. Import the data:

```python
file_location = "/FileStore/tables/train_FD001.txt"
file_type = "csv"

schema = StructType([
                StructField("engine_id", IntegerType()),
                StructField("cycle", IntegerType()),
                StructField("setting1", DoubleType()),
                StructField("setting2", DoubleType()),
                StructField("setting3", DoubleType()),
                StructField("s1", DoubleType()),
                StructField("s2", DoubleType()),
                StructField("s3", DoubleType()),
                StructField("s4", DoubleType()),
                StructField("s5", DoubleType()),
                StructField("s6", DoubleType()),
                StructField("s7", DoubleType()),
                StructField("s8", DoubleType()),
                StructField("s9", DoubleType()),
                StructField("s10", DoubleType()),
                StructField("s11", DoubleType()),
                StructField("s12", DoubleType()),
                StructField("s13", DoubleType()),
                StructField("s14", DoubleType()),
                StructField("s15", DoubleType()),
                StructField("s16", DoubleType()),
                StructField("s17", IntegerType()),
                StructField("s18", IntegerType()),
                StructField("s19", DoubleType()),
                StructField("s20", DoubleType()),
                StructField("s21", DoubleType())
```

```
                          ])

         df = spark.read.option("delimiter"," ").csv(file_location,
                                               schema=schema,
                                               header=False)
```

3. Create a table view on the data:

```
         df.createOrReplaceTempView("raw_engine")
```

4. Transform the data:

```
         %sql

         drop table if exists engine;

         create table engine as
         (select e.*, CASE WHEN mc - e.cycle = 1 THEN 1 ELSE
         CASE WHEN mc - e.cycle < 14 THEN 2 ELSE
         0 END END as label
         from raw_engine e
         join (select max(cycle) mc, engine_id from raw_engine group by
         engine_id) m
         on e.engine_id = m.engine_id)
```

5. Test, train, and split the data:

```
         new_input = spark.sql("select * from engine").toPandas()
         training_df, test_df = train_test_split(new_input)
```

6. Prepare the model:

```
         dtrain = xgb.DMatrix(training_df[['setting1','setting2','setting3',
         's1', 's2', 's3',
         's4', 's5', 's6', 's7', 's8', 's9', 's10', 's11', 's12', 's13',
         's14',
         's15', 's16','s17', 's18', 's19', 's20', 's21']],
         label=training_df["label"])
         param = {'max_depth': 2, 'eta': 1, 'silent': 1, 'objective':
         'multi:softmax'}
         param['nthread'] = 4
         param['eval_metric'] = 'auc'
         param['num_class'] = 3
```

7. Train the model:

```
         num_round = 10
         bst = xgb.train(param, dtrain, num_round)
```

8. Evaluate the model:

```
dtest = xgb.DMatrix(test_df[['setting1', 'setting2', 'setting3',
                            's1', 's2', 's3', 's4', 's5', 's6',
                            's7', 's8', 's9', 's10', 's11',
                            's12', 's13', 's14', 's15', 's16',
                            's17', 's18', 's19', 's20', 's21']])
ypred = bst.predict(dtest)

pre_score = precision_score(test_df["label"], ypred,
                            average='micro')
print("xgb_pre_score:",pre_score)
```

9. Store the results:

```
with mlflow.start_run():
    mlflow.set_experiment("/Shared/experiments/\
                          Predictive_Maintenance")
    mlflow.log_param("type", 'XGBoost')
    mlflow.log_metric("precision_score", pre_score)
    filename = 'bst.sav'
    pickle.dump(bst, open(filename, 'wb'))
    mlflow.log_artifact(filename)
```

How it works...

First, we import `pandas`, `pyspark`, and `numpy` for data wrangling, `xgboost` for our algorithm, `sklearn` for scoring our results, and finally `mlflow` and `pickle` for saving those results. In *step 2*, we specify a schema in Spark. The inferred schema feature of Databricks can often get the schema wrong. Often we need to specify data types. In the next step, we create a temp view of the data so that we can use the SQL tools in Databricks. In *step 4*, we use the magic `%sql` tag at the top of the page to change the language to SQL. We then create a table call, `engine`, that has the engine data plus a new column that gives 0 if the engine has more than 14 cycles left, 1 if it has only one cycle left, and 2 if it has 14 cycles left. We then switch back to the default Python language and split the data into test and training datasets. In *step 6*, we specify the columns in the model as well as the hyperparameters. From here we train the model. We then test our model and print the precision score. Next, we will store the results in MLflow. In `Chapter 4`, *Deep Learning for Predictive Maintenance*, we will conduct other experiments against this dataset to see which one performs best.

XGBoost has a large number of parameters you can tune. These tuning parameters can be the number of threads that algorithms are allowed to use, and tree parameters that help increase accuracy or prevent over and underfitting. Some of these include:

- `learning_rate`: The learning rate is the step size of the algorithm to update its nodes. It helps prevent overfitting but can also negatively affect how long it takes to complete the training.
- `max_depth`: A deep tree tends to overfit and a shallow tree tends to underfit.
- `predictor`: This is a flag to tell the program to do its computations on either the CPU or GPU. GPUs can dramatically increase performance time but not all computers have a GPU.

There are a dozen more parameters that can be tuned in XGBoost.

XGBoosted decision trees under the hood take weak learners or shallow trees and combine them into a strong learner using a dimension scoring system. It is similar to getting a bad diagnosis from a doctor and getting a second and third opinion. The first doctor could be wrong but it is less likely that all three doctors are wrong.

Detecting unsafe drivers

Computer vision in machine learning has allowed us to tell if there are accidents on roads or unsafe work environments and can be used in conjunction with complex systems such as smart sales assistants. Computer vision has opened up many possibilities in IoT. Computer vision is also one of the most challenging from a cost perspective. In the next two recipes, we are going to discuss two different ways of using computer vision. The first one takes in large amounts of images generated from IoT devices and performs predictions and analysis on them using the high-performance distributed Databricks format. In the next recipe, we are going to use a technique for performing machine learning on edge devices with a small amount of compute using a low compute algorithm.

Getting ready

To get ready, you will need Databricks. In the example of this recipe, we are going to pull images from Azure Blob Storage.

How to do it...

The steps for this recipe are as follows:

1. Import the libraries and configurations:

```
from pyspark.ml.classification import LogisticRegression
from pyspark.ml import Pipeline
from sparkdl import DeepImageFeaturizer
from pyspark.ml.evaluation import \
MulticlassClassificationEvaluator
from pyspark.sql.functions import lit
import pickle
import mlflow

storage_account_name = "Your Storage Account Name"
storage_account_access_key = "Your Key"
```

2. Read the data:

```
safe_images = "wasbs://unsafedrivers@"+storage_account_name+\
              ".blob.core.windows.net/safe/"
safe_df = spark.read.format('image').load(safe_images)\
        .withColumn("label", lit(0))

unsafe_images = "wasbs://unsafedrivers@"+storage_account_name+\
              ".blob.core.windows.net/unsafe/"
unsafe_df = spark.read.format('image').load(unsafe_images)\
        .withColumn("label", lit(1))
```

3. Query the data:

```
display(unsafe_df)
```

4. Create testing and training datasets:

```
unsafe_train, unsafe_test = unsafe_df.randomSplit([0.6, 0.4])
safe_train, safe_test = safe_df.randomSplit([0.6, 0.4])

train_df = unsafe_train.unionAll(safe_train)
test_df = safe_test.unionAll(unsafe_test)
```

5. Build a pipeline:

```
featurizer = DeepImageFeaturizer(inputCol="image",
                                 outputCol="features",
                                 modelName="ResNet50")
lr = LogisticRegression(maxIter=20, regParam=0.05,
                        elasticNetParam=0.3, labelCol="label")
p = Pipeline(stages=[featurizer, lr])
```

6. Train the model:

```
p_model = p.fit(train_df)
```

7. Evaluate the model:

```
predictions = p_model.transform(test_df)

predictions.select("filePath", "prediction").show(truncate=False)
df = p_model.transform(test_df)

predictionAndLabels = df.select("prediction", "label")
evaluator = \
MulticlassClassificationEvaluator(metricName="accuracy")
print("Training set accuracy = " + \
      str(evaluator.evaluate(predictionAndLabels)))
```

8. Record the results:

```
with mlflow.start_run():
    mlflow.set_experiment("/Shared/experiments/Workplace Safety")

    mlflow.log_param("Model Name", "ResNet50")
    # Log a metric; metrics can be updated throughout the run
    precision, recall, fscore, support=score(y_test, y_pred,
                                              average='macro')

    mlflow.log_metric("Accuracy", \
                      evaluator.evaluate(predictionAndLabels))

    filename = 'finalized_model.sav'
    pickle.dump(p_model, open(filename, 'wb'))
    # Log an artifact (output file)
    mlflow.log_artifact(filename)
```

How it works...

First, we are defining where the files are located. For this recipe, we are using Azure Blob Storage, but any storage system, such as S3 or HDFS, would work as well. Replace the `storage_account_name` and `storage_account_access_key` fields with the keys of your Blob Storage account. Read both *safe* and *unsafe* images in from our storage account into a Spark image DataFrame. In our example, we have placed safe images in one folder and unsafe images in another. Query the image DataFrame to see if it got the images. Create safe and unsafe test and training sets. We then union our datasets into a training set and a testing set. Next, we create a machine learning pipeline. We use the ResNet-50 algorithm as a featurizer. Next, we use logistic regression as our classifier. We then put it into a pipeline and train our model. Next, we take our pipeline and run our training DataFrame through it to come out with a trained model. We then evaluate the accuracy of our model. Finally, we store the results in MLflow so that we can compare it against other models.

There are many image classification models that have been developed, such as ResNet-50 and Inception v3. In our example, we used ResNet-50, which is a type of tuned convolutional neural network. ResNet-50 is a powerful machine learning model for image featurization. In machine learning, there is the *no free lunch theorem*, which states that no one model will outperform the rest. For this reason, data scientists will test different algorithms. This can simply be done by changing a parameter such as a metric name.

We also used a Spark ML pipeline. Pipelines allow data scientists to declare different steps of a process and implement them independently. In our case, we used ResNet-50 to featurize the image. ResNet-50 outputs a vector of features that can be classified by a classifier. In our case, we use logistic regression, but we could have used XGBoost or a different neural network.

There's more...

To change our pipeline to use Inception instead of `ResNet50`, we simply need to change the model:

```
featurizer = DeepImageFeaturizer(inputCol="image", outputCol="features",
                                 modelName="ResNet50")
```

Using `Inception v3`, we are able to test the accuracy of different models on the image set:

```
featurizer = DeepImageFeaturizer(inputCol="image", outputCol="features",
                                 modelName="InceptionV3")
```

We could use an array of models and record the results in MLflow:

```
for m in ['InceptionV3', 'Xception','ResNet50', 'VGG19']:
    featurizer = DeepImageFeaturizer(inputCol="image",
                                     outputCol="features",
                                     modelName=m)
```

Face detection on constrained devices

Deep neural networks tend to outperform other classification techniques. However, with IoT devices, there is not a large amount of RAM, compute, or storage. On constrained devices, RAM and storage are often in MB and not in GB, making traditional classifiers not possible. Some video classification services in the cloud charge over $10,000 per device for live streaming video. OpenCV's Haar classifiers have the same underlying principles as a convolutional neural network but at a fraction of the compute and storage. OpenCV is available in multiple languages and runs on some of the most constrained devices.

In this recipe, we are going to set up a Haar Cascade to detect if a person is close to the camera. This is often used in Kiosk and other interactive smart devices. The Haar Cascade can be run at a high rate of speed and when it finds a face that is close to the machine it can send that image via a cloud service or a different onboard machine learning model.

Getting ready

The first thing we need to do is install the OpenCV framework:

```
pip install opencv-python
```

Next, we download the model. The model can be downloaded from the OpenCV GitHub page or the book's GitHub page. The file is haarcascade_frontalface_default.xml.

Next, we create a new folder by importing the haarcascade_frontalface_default.xml file and creating a Python file for the code. Finally, if the device does not have a camera attached to it, attach one. In the following recipe, we are going to implement a Haar Cascade using OpenCV.

How to do it...

The steps for this recipe are as follows:

1. Import the libraries and settings:

```
import cv2
from time import sleep

debugging = True
classifier = \
cv2.CascadeClassifier("haarcascade_frontalface_default.xml")
video = cv2.VideoCapture(0)
```

2. Initialize the camera:

```
while True:
    if not video.isOpened():
    print('Waiting for Camera.')
    sleep(5)
    pass
```

3. Capture and transform the image:

```
ret, frame = video.read()
gray = cv2.cvtColor(frame, cv2.COLOR_BGR2GRAY)
```

4. Classify the image:

```
faces = classifier.detectMultiScale(gray,
                                     minNeighbors=5,
                                     minSize=(100, 100)
                                     )
```

5. Debug the images:

```
if debugging:
    # Draw a rectangle around the faces
    for (x, y, w, h) in faces:
        cv2.rectangle(frame, (x, y), (x+w, y+h), (0, 255, 0), 2)

    cv2.imshow('Video', frame)
    if cv2.waitKey(1) & 0xFF == ord('q'):
        break
```

6. Detect the face:

```
if len(faces) > 0:
    # Your advanced code here
    pass
```

How it works...

First, import the libraries and set the settings. In the next step, we import the `opencv` and `python` libraries and we also import `time` so we can wait if the camera is not ready. Next, we set some debugging flags so we can test the output visually if we are debugging. Then we import the Haar Cascade XML file into our classifier. Finally, we open the first video camera attached to the machine. In *step 2*, we wait for the camera to become ready. This is often not a problem when developing the software as the system has already recognized the camera. Then we set this program to run automatically; the camera may not be available for up to a minute when the system is restarted. We are also starting an infinite loop of processing the camera images. In the next step, we capture and transform the image into black and white. Next, we run the classifier. The `detectMultiScale` classifier allows faces of different sizes to be detected. The `minNeighbors` parameter specifies how many collaborating neighbors the detection needs before detecting a face. Making the `minNeighbors` parameter small could result in a false positive. Setting it too large may not detect a face at all. Finally, there is the minimum size in pixels that the face needs to be. To debug the code and make sure the camera is working accurately we have put in some debug code that outputs the video and a bounding box to the attached monitor. On a deployed device, this adds a considerable load. But for testing, this can reveal issues and allow tuning. If a face has been detected, then you are ready to perform tasks such as onboard sentiment analysis or send it to an external service such as the Azure Face API to identify people through a face ID.

A Haar Cascade is a highly efficient face detection classifier. Under the hood, it takes rectangular sections of the image and compares them against another part of the image to come up with something that has the characteristics of a face. In our recipe, we used the camera on the device, transformed it, and then used the Haar Cascade to classify it.

4
Deep Learning for Predictive Maintenance

Predictive maintenance is one of the most sought after machine learning solutions for IoT. It is also one of the most elusive machine learning solutions for IoT. Other areas of machine learning can easily be solved, implementing Computer Vision, for example, can be done in hours using tools such as OpenCV or Keras. To be successful with predictive maintenance you first need the right sensors. The *Data collection design* recipe in `Chapter 2`, *Handling Data*, can be used to help determine proper sensor placement. The *Exploratory factor analysts* recipe in `Chapter 2`, *Handling Data* can help determine the cadence with which the data needs to be stored. One of the biggest hurdles to implementing predictive maintenance is that there needs to be a sufficient amount of device failures. For rugged industrial devices, this can take a long time. Linking repair records with device telemetry is also a critical step.

Even though the challenge is daunting the rewards are great. A properly implemented predictive maintenance solution can save lives by helping to ensure critical devices are ready when needed. They can also increase customer loyalty because they help companies have less downtime than similar products on the market. Finally, they can reduce costs and improve efficiency by giving service technicians the information they need before servicing the device. This can help them diagnose the device and ensure that they have the right parts with them when they are servicing the device.

In this chapter, we will continue to use the NASA Turbofan dataset for predictive maintenance and cover the following recipes:

- Enhancing data using feature engineering
- Using Keras for fall detection
- Implementing LSTM to predict device failure
- Deploying models to web services

Enhancing data using feature engineering

One of the best use of time in improving models is feature engineering. The ecosystem of IoT has many tools that can make it easier. Devices can be geographically connected or hierarchically connected with digital twins, graph frames, and GraphX. This can add features such as showing the degree of contentedness to other failing devices. Windowing can show how the current reading differs over a period of time. Streaming tools such as Kafka can combine different data streams allowing you to combine data from other sources. Machines that are outdoor may be negatively affected by high temperatures or moisture as opposed to machines that are in a climate-controlled building.

In this recipe, we are going to look at enhancing our data by looking at time-series data such as deltas, seasonality, and windowing. One of the most valuable uses of time for a data scientist is feature engineering. Being able to slice the data into meaningful features can greatly increase the accuracy of our models.

Getting ready

In the *Predictive maintenance with XGBoost* recipe in the previous chapter, we used XGBoost to predict whether or not a machine needed maintenance. We have imported the NASA *Turbofan engine degradation simulation* dataset which can be found at `https://data.nasa.gov/dataset/Turbofan-engine-degradation-simulation-data-set/vrks-gjie`. In the rest of this chapter, we will continue to use that dataset. To get ready you will need the dataset.

Then if you have not already imported `numpy`, `pandas`, `matplotlib`, and `seaborn` into Databricks do so now.

How to do it...

The following steps need to be observed to follow this recipe:

1. Firstly, import the required libraries. We will be using `pyspark.sql`, `numpy`, and `pandas` for data manipulation and `matplotlib` and `seaborn` for visualization:

```
from pyspark.sql import functions as F
from pyspark.sql.window import Window

import pandas as pd
import numpy as np
np.random.seed(1385)
```

```
import matplotlib as mpl
import matplotlib.pyplot as plt
import seaborn as sns
```

2. Next, we're going to import the data and apply a schema to it so that the data types can be correctly used. To do this we import the data file through the wizard and then apply our schema to it:

```
file_location = "/FileStore/tables/train_FD001.txt"
file_type = "csv"

from pyspark.sql.types import *
schema = StructType([
  StructField("engine_id", IntegerType()),
  StructField("cycle", IntegerType()),
  StructField("setting1", DoubleType()),
  StructField("setting2", DoubleType()),
  StructField("setting3", DoubleType()),
  StructField("s1", DoubleType()),
  StructField("s2", DoubleType()),
  StructField("s3", DoubleType()),
  StructField("s4", DoubleType()),
  StructField("s5", DoubleType()),
  StructField("s6", DoubleType()),
  StructField("s7", DoubleType()),
  StructField("s8", DoubleType()),
  StructField("s9", DoubleType()),
  StructField("s10", DoubleType()),
  StructField("s11", DoubleType()),
  StructField("s12", DoubleType()),
  StructField("s13", DoubleType()),
  StructField("s14", DoubleType()),
  StructField("s15", DoubleType()),
  StructField("s16", DoubleType()),
  StructField("s17", IntegerType()),
  StructField("s18", IntegerType()),
  StructField("s19", DoubleType()),
  StructField("s20", DoubleType()),
  StructField("s21", DoubleType())
  ])
```

3. Finally, we put it into a Spark DataFrame:

```
df = spark.read.option("delimiter"," ").csv(file_location,
                                           schema=schema,
                                           header=False)
```

4. We then create a temporary view so that we can run a Spark SQL job on it:

```
df.createOrReplaceTempView("raw_engine")
```

5. Next, we calculate **remaining useful life** (**RUL**). Using the SQL magics, we create a table named `engine` from the `raw_engine` temp view we just created. We then use SQL to calculate the RUL:

```
%sql

drop table if exists engine;

create table engine as
(select e.*
,mc - e.cycle as rul
, CASE WHEN mc - e.cycle < 14 THEN 1 ELSE 0 END as
needs_maintenance
from raw_engine e
join (select max(cycle) mc, engine_id from raw_engine group by
engine_id) m
on e.engine_id = m.engine_id)
```

6. We then import the data into a Spark DataFrame:

```
df = spark.sql("select * from engine")
```

7. Now we calculate the **rate of change** (**ROC**). In the ROC calculation, we are looking at the ROC based on the current record compared to the previous record. The ROC calculation gets the percent of change between the current cycle and the previous one:

```
my_window = Window.partitionBy('engine_id').orderBy("cycle")
df = df.withColumn("roc_s9",
                    ((F.lag(df.s9).over(my_window)/df.s9) -1)*100)
df = df.withColumn("roc_s20",
                    ((F.lag(df.s20).over(my_window)/df.s20) -1)*100)
df = df.withColumn("roc_s2",
                    ((F.lag(df.s2).over(my_window)/df.s2) -1)*100)
df = df.withColumn("roc_s14",
                    ((F.lag(df.s14).over(my_window)/df.s14) -1)*100)
```

8. Next, we review static columns. In order to do that, we're going to convert the Spark DataFrame to Pandas so that we can view summary statistics on the data such as mean quartiles and standard deviation:

```
pdf = df.toPandas()
pdf.describe().transpose()
```

This will get the following output:

	count	mean	std	min	25%	50%	75%	max
engine_id	20631.0	51.506568	2.922763e+01	1.000000	26.000000	52.000000	77.000000	100.000000
cycle	20631.0	108.807862	6.888099e+01	1.000000	52.000000	104.000000	156.000000	362.000000
setting1	20631.0	-0.000009	2.187313e-03	-0.008700	-0.001500	0.000000	0.001500	0.008700
setting2	20631.0	0.000002	2.930621e-04	-0.000600	-0.000200	-0.000000	0.000300	0.000600
setting3	20631.0	100.000000	0.000000e+00	100.000000	100.000000	100.000000	100.000000	100.000000
s1	20631.0	518.670000	0.000000e+00	518.670000	518.670000	518.670000	518.670000	518.670000
s2	20631.0	642.680934	5.000533e-01	641.210000	642.325000	642.640000	643.000000	644.530000
s3	20631.0	1590.523119	6.131150e+00	1571.040000	1586.260000	1590.100000	1594.380000	1616.910000
s4	20631.0	1408.933782	9.000605e+00	1382.250000	1402.360000	1408.040000	1414.555000	1441.490000
s5	20631.0	14.620000	1.776400e-15	14.620000	14.620000	14.620000	14.620000	14.620000
s6	20631.0	21.609803	1.388985e-03	21.600000	21.610000	21.610000	21.610000	21.610000
s7	20631.0	553.367711	8.850923e-01	549.850000	552.810000	553.440000	554.010000	556.060000

9. Now we drop the columns that are not valuable to us in this exercise. For example, we are going to drop `settings3` and `s1` columns because the values never change:

```
columns_to_drop = ['s1', 's5', 's10', 's16', 's18', 's19',
                   'op_setting3', 'setting3']
df = df.drop(*columns_to_drop)
```

10. Next, we are going to review the correlation between values. We are looking for columns that are exactly the same. First, we perform a correlation function on the DataFrame. Then we use `np.zeros_like` to mask the upper triangle. We are then going to set the figure size. Next, we are going to use `diverging_palette` to define a custom color map, then we are going to use the `heatmap` function do draw the heat map:

```
corr = pdf.corr().round(1)
mask = np.zeros_like(corr, dtype=np.bool)
mask[np.triu_indices_from(mask)] = True

f, ax = plt.subplots(figsize=(20, 20))

cmap = sns.diverging_palette(220, 10, as_cmap=True)

sns.heatmap(corr, mask=mask, cmap=cmap, vmin=-1, vmax=1, center=0,
```

```
                     square=True, linewidths=.5, cbar_kws={"shrink": .5},
                     annot=True)

          display(plt.tight_layout())
```

The following heat map shows values with a high degree of correlation. The values that are 1 show that they are perfectly correlated and therefore can be dropped from the analysis:

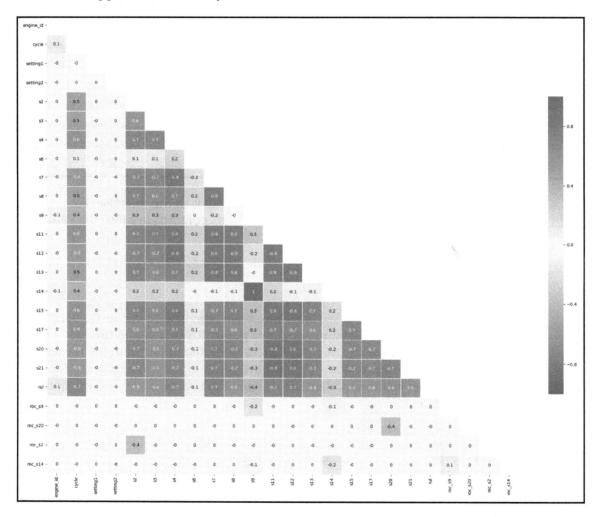

11. Remove similar columns. We found that s14 is exactly the same as s9 so we are removing that column:

```
columns_to_drop = ['s14']
df = df.drop(*columns_to_drop)
```

12. Now we take the DataFrame and express it visually. A histogram or distribution table is used to show potential issues with our data such as outliers, skew data, random data and data that would not affect the model:

```
pdf = df.toPandas()

plt.figure(figsize = (16, 8))
plt.title('Example temperature sensor', fontsize=16)
plt.xlabel('# Cycles', fontsize=16)
plt.ylabel('Degrees', fontsize=16)
plt.xticks(fontsize=16)
plt.yticks(fontsize=16)
pdf.hist(bins=50, figsize=(18,16))
display(plt.show())
```

The following histogram screenshots are the results:

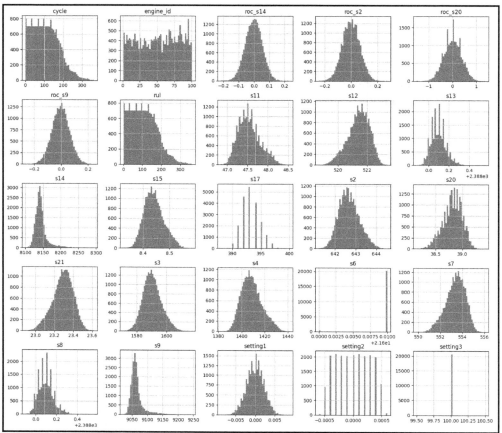

13. We then review the noise of our model to make sure that it is not unduly affected by fluctuation:

```
values = pdf[pdf.engine_id==1].values
groups = [5, 6, 7, 8, 9, 10, 11,12,13]
i = 1
plt.figure(figsize=(10,20))
for group in groups:
    plt.subplot(len(groups), 1, i)
    plt.plot(values[:, group])
    plt.title(pdf.columns[group], y=0.5, loc='right')
    i += 1
display(plt.show())
```

The following is the output:

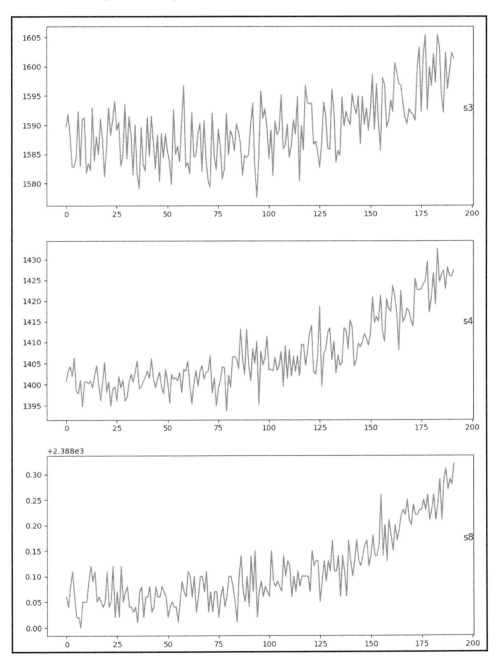

14. Based on the previous step, it is clear that the data is noisy. This can lead to false readings. A rolling average can help smooth the data. Using a 7 cycle rolling average we denoise the data as shown:

```
w = (Window.partitionBy('engine_id').orderBy("cycle")\
    .rangeBetween(-7,0))
df = df.withColumn('rolling_average_s2', F.avg("s2").over(w))
df = df.withColumn('rolling_average_s3', F.avg("s3").over(w))
df = df.withColumn('rolling_average_s4', F.avg("s4").over(w))
df = df.withColumn('rolling_average_s7', F.avg("s7").over(w))
df = df.withColumn('rolling_average_s8', F.avg("s8").over(w))

pdf = df.toPandas()
values = pdf[pdf.engine_id==1].values
groups = [5, 25, 6, 26, 8, 27]
i = 1
plt.figure(figsize=(10,20))
for group in groups:
    plt.subplot(len(groups), 1, i)
    plt.plot(values[:, group])
    plt.title(pdf.columns[group], y=0.5, loc='right')
    i += 1
display(plt.show())
```

The following screenshot is a chart of `rolling_average_s4` versus `s4`:

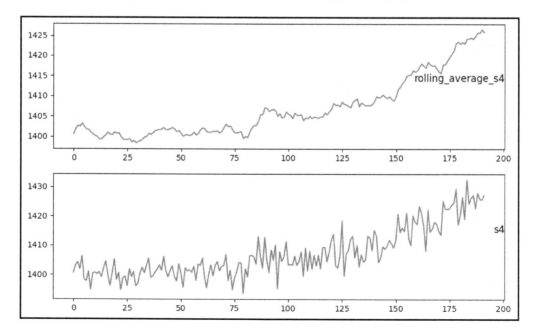

15. Since we want this data to be accessible to other notebooks, we're going to save it as an ML ready table:

```
df.write.mode("overwrite").saveAsTable("engine_ml_ready")
```

How it works...

In this recipe, we have performed feature engineering so that we could make our data more usable by our ML algorithms. We removed the columns with no variation, high correlation, and we denoised the dataset. In *step 8* we removed the columns with no variation. The method describes the data in several ways. Reviewing the chart showed that many variables do not change at all. Next, we used a heat map to find sensors that had the same data. Finally, we used a rolling average to smooth the data from our original dataset into a new one.

There's more...

So far we have just looked at training data. But we will also need to look at testing the data. There is a test dataset and a RUL dataset. These datasets will help us test our models. To import them you would run 2 additional import steps:

1. **Importing test data**: Relying on the schema from the training set the test set is imported and put in a table called `engine_test`:

```
# File location and type
file_location = "/FileStore/tables/test_FD001.txt"
df = spark.read.option("delimiter"," ").csv(file_location,
                                      schema=schema,
                                      header=False)
df.write.mode("overwrite").saveAsTable("engine_test")
```

2. **Importing the RUL Dataset**: The next step is to import the remaining useful life dataset and save that to a table as well:

```
file_location = "/FileStore/tables/RUL_FD001.txt"
RULschema = StructType([StructField("RUL", IntegerType())])
df = spark.read.option("delimiter"," ").csv(file_location,
                                      schema=RULschema,
                                      header=False)
df.write.mode("overwrite").saveAsTable("engine_RUL")
```

Using keras for fall detection

One strategy for predictive maintenance is to look at patterns of device failures for a given record. In this recipe, we will classify the data that exhibits a pattern that happens before the device fails.

We will be using `keras`, which is a fairly powerful machine learning library. Keras strips away some of the complexity of TensorFlow and PyTorch. Keras is a great framework for beginners in machine learning as it is easy to get started on and the concepts learned in Keras transfer to more expressive machine learning libraries such as TensorFlow and PyTorch.

Getting ready

This recipe expands on the predictive maintenance dataset we feature engineered in the previous recipe. If you have not already done so you will need to import the `keras`, `tensorflow`, `sklearn`, `pandas`, and `numpy` libraries into your Databricks cluster.

How to do it...

Please observe the following steps:

1. Firstly, import the required libraries. We import `pandas`, `pyspark.sql`, and `numpy` for data manipulation, `keras` for machine learning, and `sklearn` for evaluating the model. After evaluating the model we use `io`, `pickle`, and `mlflow` to save the model and results so that it can be evaluated against other models:

   ```
   from pyspark.sql.functions import *
   from pyspark.sql.window import Window

   import pandas as pd
   import numpy as np
   import io
   import keras
   from sklearn.model_selection import train_test_split
   from sklearn.metrics import precision_score
   from sklearn.preprocessing import MinMaxScaler

   from keras.models import Sequential
   from keras.layers import Dense, Activation, LeakyReLU, Dropout
   ```

```
import pickle
import mlflow
```

2. Next, we import training and testing data. Out training data will be used to train our models and our testing data will be used to evaluate the models:

```
X_train = spark.sql("select rolling_average_s2, rolling_average_s3,
                    rolling_average_s4, rolling_average_s7,
                    rolling_average_s8 from \
                    engine_ml_ready").toPandas()

y_train = spark.sql("select needs_maintenance from \
                    engine_ml_ready").toPandas()

X_test = spark.sql("select rolling_average_s2, rolling_average_s3,
                    rolling_average_s4, rolling_average_s7,
                    rolling_average_s8 from \
                    engine_test_ml_ready").toPandas()

y_test = spark.sql("select needs_maintenance from \
                    engine_test_ml_ready").toPandas()
```

3. Now we scale the data. Each sensor of the dataset has a different scale. For example, the maximum value of S1 is 518 while the maximum value of S16 is 0.03. For that reason, we convert all of the values to a range between 0 and 1. Allowing each metric affect the model in a similar way. We will make use of the MinMaxScaler function from the sklearn library to adjust the scale:

```
scaler = MinMaxScaler(feature_range=(0, 1))
X_train.iloc[:,1:6] = scaler.fit_transform(X_train.iloc[:,1:6])
X_test.iloc[:,1:6] = scaler.fit_transform(X_test.iloc[:,1:6])
dim = X_train.shape[1]
```

4. The first layer, the input layer, has 32 nodes. The activation function, LeakyReLU, defines the output node when given the input. To prevent overfitting, 25% of the layers both hidden and visible are dropped when training:

```
model = Sequential()
model.add(Dense(32, input_dim = dim))
model.add(LeakyReLU())
model.add(Dropout(0.25))
```

5. Similar to the input layer, the hidden layer, uses 32 nodes as the input layer and `LeakyReLU` as its output layer. It also uses a 25% drop out to prevent overfitting:

```
model.add(Dense(32))
model.add(LeakyReLU())
model.add(Dropout(0.25))
```

6. Finally, we add an output layer. We give it one layer so that we can have an output between 0 and 1. `sigmoid`, our activation function, helps predict the probability of the output. Our optimizer, `rmsprop`, along with the loss function helps optimize the data pattern and reduce the error rate:

```
model.add(Dense(1))
model.add(Activation('sigmoid'))
model.compile(optimizer ='rmsprop', loss ='binary_crossentropy',
            metrics = ['accuracy'])
```

7. Now we train the Model. We use the `model.fit` function to specify our training and test data. The batch size is used to set the number of training records used in 1 iteration of the algorithm. The epoch of 5 means that it will pass through the data set 5 times:

```
model.fit(X_train, y_train, batch_size = 32, epochs = 5,
            verbose = 1, validation_data = (X_test, y_test))
```

8. The next step is to evaluate the results. We use the trained model and our `X_test` dataset to get the predictions (`y_pred`). We then compare the predictions with the real results and review how accurate it is:

```
y_pred = model.predict(X_test)
pre_score = precision_score(y_test,y_pred, average='micro')
print("Neural Network:",pre_score)
```

9. Next, we save the results to `mlflow`. The results will be compared against the other ML algorithms for predictive maintenance we are using in this book:

```
with mlflow.start_run():
mlflow.set_experiment("/Shared/experiments/Predictive_Maintenance")
    mlflow.log_param("model", 'Neural Network')
    mlflow.log_param("Inputactivation", 'Leaky ReLU')
    mlflow.log_param("Hiddenactivation", 'Leaky ReLU')
    mlflow.log_param("optimizer", 'rmsprop')
    mlflow.log_param("loss", 'binary_crossentropy')
```

```
mlflow.log_metric("precision_score", pre_score)
filename = 'NeuralNet.pickel'
pickle.dump(model, open(filename, 'wb'))
mlflow.log_artifact(filename)
```

How it works...

There are typically three tasks that neural networks does:

- Import data
- Recognize the patterns of the data by training
- Predicting the outcomes of new data

Neural networks take in data, trains themselves to recognize the patterns of the data, and then are used to predict the outcomes of new data. This recipe uses the cleaned and feature engineered dataset saved in the previous recipe. The X_train dataset is pulled in from the spark data table into a Panda DataFrame. The training DataFrames, X_train, and y_train are used for training. X_test gives us a list of devices that have failed and y_test gives us the real-time failure of those machines. Those datasets are used to train models and test the results.

First, we have the input layer. The data is fed to each of our 32 input neurons. The neurons are connected through channels. The channel is assigned a numerical value known as **weight**. The inputs are multiplied by the corresponding weight and their sum is sent as input to the neurons in the hidden layer. Each of these neurons is associated with a numerical value called the **bias**, which is added to the input sum. This value is then passed to a threshold function called the **activation function**. The activation function determines if a neuron will get activated or not. We used Leaky ReLU as our activation function for our first 2 layers. **ReLU** or **Rectified Linear Unit** is a popular activation function because it solves the vanishing gradient problem. In this recipe, we used the Leaky ReLU. Leaky ReLU solves a problem that ReLU has where big gradients can cause the neuron to never fire. The activated neuron passes its data to the next layer over the channels. This method allows the data to be propagated through the network. This is called **forward propagation**. In the output layer, the neuron with the highest layer fires and determines the output.

When we first start running data through our network, the data usually has a high degree of error. Our error and optimizer functions use backpropagation to update the weights. The cycle of forward propagation and backpropagation is repeated to achieve a lower error rate. The following diagram shows how the input, hidden, and output layers are linked together:

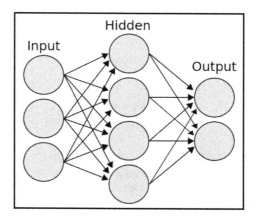

There's more...

In this recipe, we used `LeakyReLU` as our activation function, `rmsprop` as our optimizer, and `binary_crossentropy` as our loss function. We then saved the results to `mlflow`. We can tune parameters in this experiment by trying different combinations such as the number of neurons or the number of layers. We could also change the activation function to use ReLU or TanH. We could also use `Adam` as our optimizer. Saving those results to `mlflow` allows us to improve our model.

Implementing LSTM to predict device failure

Recurrent neural networks predict sequences of data. In the previous recipe, we looked at 1 point in time and determined to determine if maintenance was needed. As we saw in the first recipe when we did the data analysis the turbofan run to failure dataset is highly variable. The data reading at any point in time might indicate a need for maintenance while the next indicates that there is no need for maintenance. When determining whether or not to send a technician out having an oscillating signal can be problematic. **Long Short Term Memory (LSTM)** is often used with time-series data such as the turbofan run to failure dataset.

With the LSTM, we look at a series of data, similar to windowing. LSTM uses an ordered sequence to help determine, in our case, if a turbofan engine is about to fail based on the previous sequence of data.

Getting ready

For this recipe we will use the NASA *Turbofan run to failure* dataset. For this recipe we will be using a Databricks notebook. This recipe requires a few libraries to be installed. For data processing we need to install `numpy` and `pandas`, `keras` for creating a LSTM model, and `sklearn` and `mlflow` for evaluating and saving the results of our model.

Even though in previous recipes we added windowing and preprocessed the data, in this recipe we will use the raw data. LSTMs window the data and also have a good deal of extraction and transformation that is unique to this type of ML Algorithm.

How to do it...

We will execute the following steps for this recipe:

1. First, we will import all of the libraries which we will need later. We will import `pandas` and `numpy` for data processing, `keras` for the ML models, `sklearn` for evaluations, and `pickel` and `mlflow` for storing the results:

```
import pandas as pd
import numpy as np

import keras
from keras.models import Sequential
from keras.layers import Dense, Dropout, LSTM, Activation

from sklearn import preprocessing
from sklearn.metrics import confusion_matrix, recall_score,
precision_score
import pickle
import mlflow
```

2. Next we will set the variables. We will set 2 cycles periods. In addition we use a sequence length variable. The sequence length allows the LSTM to look back over 5 cycles. This is similar to windowing that was discussed in Chapter 1, *Setting Up the IoT and AI Environment*. We are also going to get a list of data columns:

```
week1 = 7
week2 = 14
sequence_length = 100
sensor_cols = ['s' + str(i) for i in range(1,22)]
sequence_cols = ['setting1', 'setting2', 'setting3', 'cycle_norm']
sequence_cols.extend(sensor_cols)
```

3. Next we import data from the spark data tables we created in the *Simple predictive maintenance with XGBoost* recipe in Chapter 3, *Machine Learning for IoT*. We also drop the label column because we are going to recalculate the labels. We are going to import three DataFrames. The train DataFrame is used to train the model. The test DataFrame is used to test the accuracy of the model and the truth DataFrame is the actual failures for the test DataFrame:

```
train = spark.sql("select * from engine").toPandas()
train.drop(columns="label" , inplace=True)
test = spark.sql("select * from engine_test2").toPandas()
truth = spark.sql("select * from engine_rul").toPandas()
```

4. Then, we generate labels that show if a device needs maintenance. label1 shows when a device will fail in 14 cycles and label2 shows when a device will fail in 7 cycles. First we create a DataFrame that shows the RUL based on the maximum cycle number for each engine. Next we use that the RUL DataFrame create a RUL column in our train DataFrame. We do this by subtracting the maximum life from the current cycle. We then drop our max column. Next we create a new column label1. label1 has a 1 value if the RUL is less than the 14 cycles. Then copy that over to label2 and add a 2 value if the RUL is less than 1 week:

```
rul = pd.DataFrame(train.groupby('engine_id')['cycle']\
                  .max()).reset_index()
rul.columns = ['engine_id', 'max']
train = train.merge(rul, on=['engine_id'], how='left')
train['RUL'] = train['max'] - train['cycle']
train.drop('max', axis=1, inplace=True)
train['label1'] = np.where(train['RUL'] <= week2, 1, 0 )
train['label2'] = train['label1']
train.loc[train['RUL'] <= week1, 'label2'] = 2
```

5. In addition to generating labels for training data we also need to do so for test data. The training and test data are slightly different. The training data had an end date that signified when the machine broke. The training set does not. Instead we have a `truth` DataFrame that shows when the machine actually failed. To add the label columns we need to combine the `test` and `truth` dataset before we can calculate the labels:

```
rul = pd.DataFrame(test.groupby('engine_id')['cycle'].max())\
                    .reset_index()
rul.columns = ['engine_id', 'max']
truth.columns = ['more']
truth['engine_id'] = truth.index + 1
truth['max'] = rul['max'] + truth['more']
truth.drop('more', axis=1, inplace=True)

test = test.merge(truth, on=['engine_id'], how='left')
test['RUL'] = test['max'] – test['cycle']
test.drop('max', axis=1, inplace=True)

test['label1'] = np.where(test['RUL'] <= week2, 1, 0 )
test['label2'] = test['label1']
test.loc[test['RUL'] <= week1, 'label2'] = 2
```

6. Next, because the columns have different mins and maxes, we will normalize the data so that one variable does not overshadow the rest. To do this we are going to use the `sklearn` library's `MinMaxScaler` function. This function transforms the values between 0 and 1. It is a great scalier to use when, as in our case, there is not a lot of outlier values. We are going to do the same normalization step for both the training and test set:

```
train['cycle_norm'] = train['cycle']
cols_normalize =
train.columns.difference(['engine_id','cycle','RUL',
                                    'label1','label2'])
min_max_scaler = preprocessing.MinMaxScaler()
norm_train = \
pd.DataFrame(min_max_scaler.fit_transform(train[cols_normalize]),
                                    columns=cols_normalize,
                                    index=train.index)
join = \
train[train.columns.difference(cols_normalize)].join(norm_train)
train = join.reindex(columns = train.columns)

test['cycle_norm'] = test['cycle']
norm_test = \
pd.DataFrame(min_max_scaler.transform(test[cols_normalize]),
```

```
                                        columns=cols_normalize,
                                        index=test.index)
test_join = \
test[test.columns.difference(cols_normalize)].join(norm_test)
test = test_join.reindex(columns = test.columns)
test = test.reset_index(drop=True)
```

7. The LSTM algorithm in Keras requires the data to be in a sequence. In our
   variables section, we chose to have `sequence_length` equal to `100`. This is one
   of the hyperparameters that can be tuned during experimentation. As this is a
   look at data over a sequential period of time the sequence length is the length of
   the sequence of data we are training the model on. There is no real rule of thumb
   on what is the optimal length for a sequence. But from experimentation, it
   became clear that small sequences were less accurate. To aid in generating our
   sequence we use the function to return the sequential data in a way that the
   LSTM algorithm expects:

```
def gen_sequence(id_df, seq_length, seq_cols):
    data_array = id_df[seq_cols].values
    num_elements = data_array.shape[0]
    for start, stop in zip(range(0, num_elements-seq_length),
                            range(seq_length, num_elements)):
        yield data_array[start:stop, :]

seq_gen = (list(gen_sequence(train[train['engine_id']==engine_id],
                            sequence_length, sequence_cols))
          for engine_id in train['engine_id'].unique())

seq_array = np.concatenate(list(seq_gen)).astype(np.float32)
```

8. The next step is to build a neural network. We build the first layer of our LSTM.
   We start off with a sequential model. Then give it the input shape and length of
   the sequence. The units tell us the dimensionality of the output shape which it
   will pass to the next layer. Next, it returns either `true` or `false`. We then add
   `Dropout` to add the randomness to our training that prevents overfitting:

```
nb_features = seq_array.shape[2]
nb_out = label_array.shape[1]

model = Sequential()

model.add(LSTM(input_shape=(sequence_length, nb_features),
              units=100, return_sequences=True))
model.add(Dropout(0.25))
```

9. We then build the network's hidden layer. Similar to the first layer the hidden layer is an LSTM layer. If, however, instead of passing the entire sequence state to the output just passes the last nodes' values:

```
model.add(LSTM(units=50, return_sequences=False))
model.add(Dropout(0.25))
```

10. Then, we build the network's output layer. The output layer specifies the output dimensions and the `activation` function. With this we have built the shape of our neural network:

```
model.add(Dense(units=nb_out, activation='sigmoid'))
```

11. Next, we run the `compile` method which configures the model for training. In it we put the metric we are evaluating against. In this case, we are measuring against `accuracy`. We then define our measure of error or loss. In this example, we are using `binary_crossentropy` as our measure. Finally, we specify the optimizer that will reduce error every iteration:

```
model.compile(loss='binary_crossentropy', optimizer='adam',
              metrics=['accuracy'])
print(model.summary())
```

12. We then use our `fit` function to train the model. Our `epochs` parameters means that the data will be run through 10 times. Because of the random dropout, the extra runs will increase accuracy. We are using `batch_size` of 200. This means that model will train through 200 samples before it updates the gradients. Next, we use `validation_split` to put 95% of the data to training the model and 5% to validating the model. Finally, we use an `EarlyStopping` callback to stop the model from training when it stops improving accuracy:

```
model.fit(seq_array, label_array, epochs=10, batch_size=200,
          validation_split=0.05, verbose=1,
          callbacks = \
          [keras.callbacks.EarlyStopping(monitor='val_loss',
                                         min_delta=0, patience=0,
                                         verbose=0, mode='auto')])
```

13. Next, we evaluate our model based on the 95%/5% split we performed on the training data. The results show our model is evaluating the 5% data that we held back at an 87% accuracy:

```
scores = model.evaluate(seq_array, label_array, verbose=1,
                        batch_size=200)
print('Accuracy: {}'.format(scores[1]))
```

14. Next, we look at the confusion matrix which shows us a matrix of correct or wrong assessments of whether the engine needed maintenance or not:

```
y_pred = model.predict_classes(seq_array,verbose=1, batch_size=200)
y_true = label_array
print('Confusion matrix\n- x-axis is true labels.\n- y-axis is
predicted labels')
cm = confusion_matrix(y_true, y_pred)
cm
```

Our confusion matrix looks like the following grid:

	Actually Did not need maintenance	Predicted Needed Maintenance
Actually Did not need maintenance	13911	220
Actually Needed Maintenance	201	1299

15. We then compute the precision and recall. Because the dataset is unbalanced, meaning there are far more values that do not need maintenance than they do, precision and recall are the most appropriate measures for evaluating this algorithm:

```
precision = precision_score(y_true, y_pred)
recall = recall_score(y_true, y_pred)
print( 'precision = ', precision, '\n', 'recall = ', recall)
```

16. Next, we need to transform the data so that the testing data is the same type of sequential data that the training data is. To do this we perform a data transformation step similar to the one we did for the training data:

```
seq_array_test_last = [test[test['engine_id']==engine_id]\
[sequence_cols].values[-sequence_length:] for engine_id in \
test['engine_id'].unique() if \
len(test[test['engine_id']==engine_id]) >= sequence_length]

seq_array_test_last = \
np.asarray(seq_array_test_last).astype(np.float32)

y_mask = [len(test[test['engine_id']==engine_id]) >= \
        sequence_length for engine_id in \
        test['engine_id'].unique()]

label_array_test_last = \
test.groupby('engine_id')['label1'].nth(-1)[y_mask].values
label_array_test_last = label_array_test_last.reshape(
    label_array_test_last.shape[0],1).astype(np.float32)
```

17. Next, we evaluate the model generated with the training dataset against the test dataset to see how accurately the model predicts when an engine needs maintenance:

```
scores_test = model.evaluate(seq_array_test_last,
                             label_array_test_last, verbose=2)
print('Accuracy: {}'.format(scores_test[1]))
y_pred_test = model.predict_classes(seq_array_test_last)
y_true_test = label_array_test_last
print('Confusion matrix\n- x-axis is true labels.\n- y-axis is
predicted labels')
cm = confusion_matrix(y_true_test, y_pred_test)
print(cm)

pre_score = precision_score(y_true_test, y_pred_test)
recall_test = recall_score(y_true_test, y_pred_test)
f1_test = 2 * (pre_score * recall_test) / (pre_score + recall_test)
print('Precision: ', pre_score, '\n', 'Recall: ', recall_test,
      '\n', 'F1-score:', f1_test )
```

18. Now that we have our results we store those along with the model in our MLflow database:

```
with mlflow.start_run():
mlflow.set_experiment("/Shared/experiments/Predictive_Maintenance")
    mlflow.log_param("type", 'LSTM')
    mlflow.log_metric("precision_score", pre_score)
    filename = 'model.sav'
    pickle.dump(model, open(filename, 'wb'))
    mlflow.log_artifact(filename)
```

How it works...

A LSTM is a special type of **recurrent neural network (RNN)**. A RNN is a neural network architecture that deal with sequenced data by keeping the sequence in memory. Conversely, a typical feed-forward neural does not keep the information about the sequences and do not allow for flexible inputs and outputs. A recursive neural network uses recursion to call from one output back to its input thereby generating a sequence. It passes a copy of the state of the network at any given time. In our case we are using two layers for our RNN. This additional layer helps with accuracy.

LSTMs solve a problem of vanilla RNNs by dropping out data to solve the vanishing gradient problem. The vanishing gradient problem is when the neural network stops training early but is inaccurate. By using dropout data we can help solve that problem. The LSTM does this by using gating functions.

Deploying models to web services

Deployment of the model can be different depending on the capabilities of the device. Some devices with extra compute can handle having the machine learning models run directly on the device. While others require assistance. In this chapter, we are going to deploy the model to a simple web service. With modern cloud web apps or Kubernetes these web services can scale to meet the needs of the fleet of devices. In the next chapter, we will show how to run the model on the device.

Getting ready

So far in this book, we have looked at three different machine learning algorithms to solve the predictive maintenance problem with the NASA Turbofan run to failure dataset. We recorded the results to MLflow. We can see that our XGBoost notebook outperformed the more complex neural networks. The following screenshot shows the MLflow result set showing the parameters and their associated scores.

Source	Versi...	Tags	Parameters	Metrics
🗎 Predic...			type: XGBoost	▼precision_score: 0.972082202404...
🗎 Deep ...			type: LSTM	▼precision_score: 0.888888888888...
🗎 Deep ...			type: LSTM	▼precision_score: 0.888888888888...
🗎 Deep ...			type: LSTM	▼precision_score: 0.875

From here we can download our model and put it in our web service. To do this we are going to use a Python Flask web service and Docker to make the service portable. Before we start, `pip install` the python `Flask` package. Also install Docker onto your local computer. Docker is a tool that allows you to build out complex deployments.

How to do it...

In this project, you will need to create three files for testing the predictor web service and one file to scale it to production. First create `app.py` for our web server, `requirements.txt` for the dependencies, and the XGBoost model you downloaded from `mlflow`. These files will allow you to test the web service. Next, to put it into production you will need to dockerize the application. Dockerizing the file allow you to deploy it to services such as cloud-based web application or Kubernetes services. These services scale easily making onboarding new IoT devices seamless. Then execute the following steps:

1. The `app.py` file is the Flask application. Import `Flask` for the web service, `os` and `pickle` for reading the model into memory, `pandas` for data manipulation, and `xgboost` to run our model:

```
from flask import Flask, request, jsonify
import os
import pickle
import pandas as pd
import xgboost as xgb
```

2. Next is to initialize our variables. By loading the Flask application and XGBoost model into memory outside a function we ensure that it only loads once rather than on every web service call. By doing this we greatly increase the speed and efficiency of the web service. We use `pickle` to re-hydrate our model. `pickle` can take almost any Python object and write it to disk. It can also, as in our case, read if from disk and put it back into memory:

```
application = Flask(__name__)
model_filename = os.path.join(os.getcwd(), 'bst.sav')
loaded_model = pickle.load(open(model_filename, "rb"))
```

3. We then create `@application.route` to give us an `http` endpoint. The `POST` methods section specifies that it will only accept post web request. We also specify that the URL will route to `/predict`. For example, when we run this locally we could use the `http://localhost:8000/precict` URL to post our JSON string. We then convert it into a `pandas` DataFrame and then an XGBoost data matrix becomes calling `predict`. We then determine if it is above `.5` or below and return the results:

```
@application.route('/predict', methods=['POST'])
def predict():
    x_test = pd.DataFrame(request.json)
    y_pred = loaded_model.predict(xgb.DMatrix(x_test))
    y_pred[y_pred > 0.5] = 1
```

```
y_pred[y_pred <= 0.5] = 0
return int(y_pred[0])
```

4. Finally, the last thing to do in any Flask app is to call the `application.run` method. This method allows us to specify a host. In this case, we are specifying a special host of `0.0.0.0` which tells flask to accept requests from other computers. Next, we specify a port. The port can be any number. It does however need to match the port in the Dockerfile:

```
if __name__ == '__main__':
    application.run(host='0.0.0.0', port=8000)
```

5. We then create a requirements file. The `requirements.txt` file will install all of the python dependencies for the project. The docker will use this to install the dependencies:

```
flask
pandas
xgboost
pickle-mixin
gunicorn
```

6. Then, we create the Dockerfile. The `docker` file allows the deployment of the predictor to a web endpoint. The first line of the docker file will pull in the official python 3.7.5 image from Docker Hub. Next, we copy the local folder to a new folder in the docker container in a folder named `app`. Next, we set the working directory to the `app` folder. Then we use `pip install` to install the requirements from the file we created in *step 5*. Then we expose port `8000`. Finally, we run the `gunicorn` command that starts the Gunicorn server:

```
FROM python:3.7.5
ADD . /app
WORKDIR /app

RUN pip install -r requirements.txt

EXPOSE 8000
CMD ["gunicorn", "-b", "0.0.0.0:8000", "app"]
```

How it works...

Flask is a lightweight web server. We pull in the model that we saved to disk using `pickle` to rehydrate the model. We then create an `http` endpoint to call into.

There's more...

Modern cloud-based web applications such as **Azure Web Apps** can automatically pull new Docker images into production. There is also a great deal of DevOps tools that can pull images and run them through various tests before deploying them with Docker container instances or docker orchestration tools such as Kubernetes. But for them to do this one must first put them into a container registry such as **Azure Container Registry** or **Docker Hub**. To do this we will need to do a few steps. First, we will build our container. Next, we can run our container to ensure that it works. Then we log into our container registry service and push the container to it. The detailed steps are as follows:

1. First, we build the container. To do it we navigate to the folder with the docker file and run docker build. We are going to tag it with the -t command to ch4. We then specify that the docker file is in the local folder with the period .:

   ```
   docker build -t ch4 .
   ```

2. Now that we have a docker image built, we are going to run the container based on the image with the docker run command. We are going to use the -it interactive command so we can see any output from the server. We are also going to use the -p or port command to specify that we are mapping the docker containers internal port 8000 to the external port 8000:

   ```
   docker run -it -p 8000:8000 ch4
   ```

3. We then need to put the container into something that can be accessible by our compute resource. To do this, first register for a Docker Registry service such as Docker Hub or Azure Container Registry. Then create a new repository. The repository provider will give you a path for that repository.

4. Next is to log in to your container registry service, tag the container, and push the container. Remember to replace [Your container path] with the registry name or path provided by the registry service:

   ```
   docker login

   docker tag ch4 [Your container path]:v1
   docker push [Your container path]:v1
   ```

You can then use docker enabled cloud technology to push that predictor service into production. Your device can then send its sensor reading to the web service and receive through a cloud to device message whether the device needs maintenance or not.

5
Anomaly Detection

diarizationThe predictive/prescriptive AI life cycle of a device starts with data collection design. Data is analyzed for factors such as correlation and variance. Then the devices start being manufactured. Other than a small number of sample devices, there is usually no device failures, that produce machine learning models. To compensate for this, most manufacturers use duty cycle thresholds to determine whether a device is in a good state or a bad state. These duty cycle standards may be that that the device is running too hot or an arbitrary value is put on a sensor for an alert. But the data quickly needs more advanced analysis. The sheer volume of data can be daunting for an individual. The analyst needs to look through millions of records to find the proverbial needle in a haystack. Using an analyst-in-the-middle approach using anomaly detection can efficiently help to find issues with devices. Anomaly detection is done through statistical, unsupervised, or supervised machine learning techniques. In other words, typically an analyst starts out looking at a single data point that is being examined for things such as spikes and dips. Then, multiple data points are pulled into an unsupervised learning model that clusters the data, allowing the data scientist to see when a set of values or patterns is not like the other sets of values. Finally, after enough device failures happen, the analyst can use the same type of machine learning we would use for predictive maintenance. Some machine learning algorithms, such as isolated forest, are better suited for anomaly detection, but the principles are the same.

Anomaly detection can be carried out before enough data is collected for supervised learning, or it can be part of a continuous monitoring solution. Anomaly detection can, for example, alert you to production issues with different factories. When an electrical engineer hands over a physical design to a factory, they perform a **bill of material** (**BOM**) optimization. In short, they alter the design to be one that can be put together more easily, or one that is more cost effective. Most physical devices are produced for a decade. In that time, parts that existed when the devices were first made may not be available, which means changes are needed to the BOM. Moving to a new manufacturer will also change the design as they produce their own BOM optimization. Anomaly detection can help pinpoint new issues popping up within your fleet.

There are many ways of looking at anomaly detection. In `Chapter 3`, *Machine Learning for IoT*, in *Analyzing chemical sensors with anomaly detection* recipe, we used K-means, a popular anomaly detection algorithm, to determine whether the chemical signature of a food item was different from the air. That is just one type of anomaly detection. There are many different types of anomaly detection. Some are specific to a particular machine and look at something that is abnormal over a period of time. Other anomaly detection algorithms look at a device acting normally and abnormally using supervised learning. Some devices are affected by their local environments or seasonality. Finally, in this chapter, we are going to talk about deploying anomaly detection to the edge.

The following recipes are included in this chapter:

- Using Z-Spikes on a Raspberry Pi and Sense HAT
- Using autoencoders to detect anomalies in labeled data
- Using isolated forest for unlabeled datasets
- Detecting time series anomalies with Luminol
- Detecting seasonality-adjusted anomalies
- Detecting spikes with streaming analytics
- Detecting anomalies on the edge

Using Z-Spikes on a Raspberry Pi and Sense HAT

Spikes or sudden changes to an individual device can warrant an alert. IoT devices are often subject to movement and weather. They can be affected by times of day or seasons of the year. The fleet of devices could be spread out throughout the world. Trying to get clear insights across the entire fleet can be challenging. Using a machine learning algorithm that incorporates the entire fleet enables us to treat each device separately.

Use cases for Z-Spikes can be a sudden discharge of batteries or a sudden temperature increase. People use Z-Spikes to tell whether something has been jostled or is suddenly vibrating. Z-Spikes can be used on pumps to see whether there is a blockage. Because Z-Spikes do so well across non-homologous environments, they are often a great candidate for edge deployments.

Getting ready

In this recipe, we are going to deploy Z-Spikes on a Raspberry Pi with a Sense HAT. The hardware itself is a fairly common development board and sensor setup for people learning about IoT. In fact, students can send their code to the International Space Station to be run on their Raspberry Pi and Sense HAT. If you do not have the equipment, there is an alternative code in the GitHub repository that simulates the device.

Once you have powered on your Raspberry Pi and attached your Sense HAT, you will need to install SciPy. In Python, you can usually install everything you need with `pip`, but in this case, you will need to install it through the Linux operating system. To do this, run the following commands in a terminal window:

```
sudo apt update
apt-cache show python3-scipy
sudo apt install -y python3-scipy
```

You will then need to `pip` install `numpy`, `kafka`, and `sense_hat`. You will also need to set up Kafka on a PC. There are instructions in Chapter 1, *Setting up the IoT and AI Environment*, in the *Setting up Kafka* recipe. Do not try to set up Kafka on the Raspberry Pi as it requires too much memory. Instead, set it up on a PC.

For the Raspberry Pi, you will need to connect a monitor, keyboard, and mouse. There is a Python editor in the developer tools menu. You will also need to know the IP address of the Kafka service.

How to do it...

The steps for this recipe are as follows:

1. Import the libraries:

   ```
   from scipy import stats
   import numpy as np
   from sense_hat import SenseHat
   import json
   from kafka import KafkaProducer
   import time
   ```

2. Wait for Sense HAT to register with the OS:

   ```
   time.sleep(60)
   ```

3. Initialize the variables:

```
device= "Pi1"
server = "[the address of the kafka server]:9092"
producer = KafkaProducer(bootstrap_servers=server)
sense = SenseHat()
sense.set_imu_config(False, True, True)
gyro = []
accel = []
```

4. Create a Z-score helper function:

```
def zscore(data):
    return np.abs(stats.zscore(np.array(data)))[0]
```

5. Create a `sendAlert` helper function:

```
def sendAlert(lastestGyro,latestAccel):
    alert = {'Gyro':lastestGyro, 'Accel':latestAccel}
    message = json.dumps(alert)
    producer.send(device+'alerts', key=bytes("alert",
                                         encoding='utf-8'),
                  value=bytes(message, encoding='utf-8'))
```

6. Create a `combined_value` helper function:

```
def combined_value(data):
    return float(data['x'])+float(data['y'])+float(data['z'])
```

7. Run the `main` function:

```
if __name__ == '__main__':
    x = 0
    while True:
        gyro.insert(0,sense.gyro_raw)
        accel.insert(0,sense.accel_raw)
        if x > 1000:
            gyro.pop()
            accel.pop()
        time.sleep(1)
        x = x + 1
        if x > 120:
            if zscore(gyro) > 4 or zscore(accel) > 4:
                sendAlert(gyro[0],accel[0])
```

How it works...

This algorithm is checking whether the last record is more than 4 standard deviations (σ) from the preceding 1,000 values. 4σ should have an anomaly 1 in every 15,787 readings or once every 4 hours. If we were to change that to 4.5 it would be once every 40 hours.

We import `scipy` for our Z-score evaluation and `numpy` for data manipulation. We then add the script to the Raspberry Pi startup so that the script will start automatically whenever there is a power reset. The machine needs to wait for peripherals, such as the Sense HAT initialization. The 60-second delay allows the OS to be aware of the Sense HAT before trying to initialize it. Then we initialize our variables. These variables are the device name, the IP address of the Kafka server, and the Sense HAT. Then we enable the Sense HAT's **internal measuring units** (**IMUs**). We disable the compass and enable the gyroscope and accelerometer. Finally, we create two arrays to put the data in. Next, we create a Z-score helper function into which we can input an array of values to return the Z-scores. Next, we need a function that we can use to send the alerts. The `sense.gyro_raw` function gets the most recent gyroscope and accelerometer reading and puts them into a Python object. It then converts it to JSON. We then create a key value that is UTF-8 byte encoded. Similarly, we encode the message payload. Next, we create a Kafka topic name. Then, we send the key and message to the topic. We then check under __main__ to see whether we are running the current file from a command shell. If we are, then we set a counter called x to 0. Then we start an infinite loop. Then we start putting in the gyroscope and accelerometer data. We then check whether the array has 1,000 elements in it. If so, we remove the last value in the array so that we keep the array small. We then increment our counter to accumulate 2 minutes of data. Finally, we check whether we are over 4 standard deviations away from the 1,000 values from our array; if so, we send our alert.

While this is a great way of looking at a device, we may want to do anomaly detection across our entire fleet. In the next recipes, we are going to create a message sender and receiver. If we were to do this in this recipe, we would make a Kafka producer message to send data on every iteration of our loop.

Using autoencoders to detect anomalies in labeled data

If you have labeled data, you can train a model to detect whether the data is normal or abnormal. For example, reading the current of an electric motor can show when extra drag is put on the motor by such things as failing ball bearings or other failing hardware. In IoT, anomalies can be a previously known phenomenon or a new event that has not been seen before. As the name suggests, autoencoders take in data and encode it to an output. With anomaly detection, we see whether a model can determine whether data is non-anomalous. In this recipe, we are going to use a Python object detection library called `pyod`.

Getting ready

In this recipe, we are going to use data gathered from the motion sensors on our Sense HAT. The final recipe in this chapter shows how to generate this dataset. We have also put this labeled dataset in the GitHub repository for this book. We are going to use a Python outlier detection framework called `pyod` or **Python Outlier Detection**. It wraps TensorFlow and performs various machine learning algorithms, such as autoencoders and isolated forests.

How to do it...

The steps for this recipe are as follows:

1. Import the libraries:

```
from pyod.models.auto_encoder import AutoEncoder
from pyod.utils.data import generate_data
from pyod.utils.data import evaluate_print
import numpy as np
import pickle
```

2. Load text files into our notebooks using NumPy arrays:

```
X_train = np.loadtxt('X_train.txt', dtype=float)
y_train = np.loadtxt('y_train.txt', dtype=float)
X_test = np.loadtxt('X_test.txt', dtype=float)
y_test = np.loadtxt('y_test.txt', dtype=float)
```

3. Use the autoencoder algorithm to fix the model to the dataset:

```
clf = AutoEncoder(epochs=30)
clf.fit(X_train)
```

4. Get the prediction scores:

```
y_test_pred = clf.predict(X_test) # outlier labels (0 or 1)
y_test_scores = clf.decision_function(X_test) # outlier scores
evaluate_print('AutoEncoder', y_test, y_test_scores)
```

5. Save the model:

```
pickle.dump( clf, open( "autoencoder.p", "wb" ) )
```

How it works...

First, we import `pyod`, our Python object detection library. Then we import `numpy` for data manipulation and `pickle` for saving our model. Next, we use `numpy` to load our data. Then we train our model and get the prediction scores. Finally, we save our model.

An autoencoder takes data as input and reduces the number of nodes through a smaller hidden layer that forces it to reduce the dimensionality. The target output for an autoencoder is the input. This allows us to use machine learning to train a model on what is non-anomalous. We can then determine how far a value falls away from the trained model. These values would be anomalous. The following diagram shows conceptually how data is coded into a set of inputs. Then, its dimensionality is reduced in the hidden layer and, finally, is outputted into a larger set of outputs:

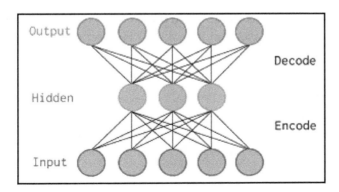

There's more...

After training our model, we need to know at what level to send the alert. When training, setting the contamination (see the following code) determines the proportion of outliers in the data that are needed to trigger the alerting function:

```
AutoEncoder(epochs=30, contamination=0.2)
```

We could also change the regularizer, as in the following example. The regularizer is used to balance the bias and variance to prevent over and underfitting:

```
AutoEncoder(epochs=30, l2_regularizer=0.2)
```

We could also change the number of neurons, our loss function, or the optimizer. This is often referred to as changing or tuning the hyperparameters in data science. Tuning the hyperparameters allows us to affect our success metrics, thereby improving the model.

Using isolated forest for unlabeled datasets

Isolated forest is a popular machine learning algorithm for anomaly detection. Isolated forests can assist in complex data models that have overlapping values. An isolated forest is an ensemble regression. Rather than using a clustering or distance-based algorithm like other machine learning algorithms, it separates outlying data points from normal data points. It does this by building a decision tree and calculates a score based on node count traversal in its path decision tree of where the data lies. In other words, it counts the number of nodes it traverses to determine an outcome. The more data that has been trained on a model, the more nodes an isolated forest would need to traverse.

Similar to the previous recipe, we are going to use pyod to easily train a model. We are going to use the Sense HAT dataset that is in the GitHub repository.

Getting ready

If you have completed the previous recipe on autoencoders, then you have everything you need. In this recipe, we are using pyod for our object detection library. The training dataset and the test dataset are in the GitHub repository for this book.

How to do it...

The steps for this recipe are as follows:

1. Import the libraries:

```
from pyod.models.iforest import IForest
from pyod.utils.data import generate_data
from pyod.utils.data import evaluate_print
import numpy as np
import pickle
```

2. Upload the data:

```
X_train = np.loadtxt('X_train.txt', dtype=float)
y_train = np.loadtxt('y_train.txt', dtype=float)
X_test = np.loadtxt('X_test.txt', dtype=float)
y_test = np.loadtxt('y_test.txt', dtype=float)
```

3. Train the model:

```
clf = IForest()
clf.fit(X_train)
```

4. Evaluate against the test data:

```
y_test_pred = clf.predict(X_test) # outlier labels (0 or 1)
y_test_scores = clf.decision_function(X_test)
print(y_test_pred)

# evaluate and print the results
print("\nOn Test Data:")
evaluate_print('IForest', y_test, y_test_scores)
```

5. Save the model:

```
pickle.dump( clf, open( "IForest.p", "wb" ) )
```

How it works...

First, we import `pyod`. We then import `numpy` for data processing and `pickle` for saving our model. Next, we perform the isolated forest training. Then we evaluate our results. We get two different types of results: one is a 1 or 0 to determine whether it is normal or anomalous, and the second gives us a score of the test. Finally, we save our model.

The isolated forest algorithm segments the data using a tree-based approach. The more clustered the data is, the more segmented it is. The isolated forest algorithm looks for the data that is not part of the dense segmented area by counting the amounts of segments it would need to traverse to get there.

There's more...

Anomaly detection is one of those analysis techniques where visualization can help us determine which hyperparameters and algorithms to use. scikit-learn has an example of how to do this on their website (`https://scikit-learn.org/stable/auto_examples/ miscellaneous/plot_anomaly_comparison.html`). A reference to this is in the GitHub repository of this book. The diagram that follows is an example of anomaly detection using multiple algorithms and settings on a toy dataset. There is no right answer in anomaly detection, but only what works best for the problem at hand:

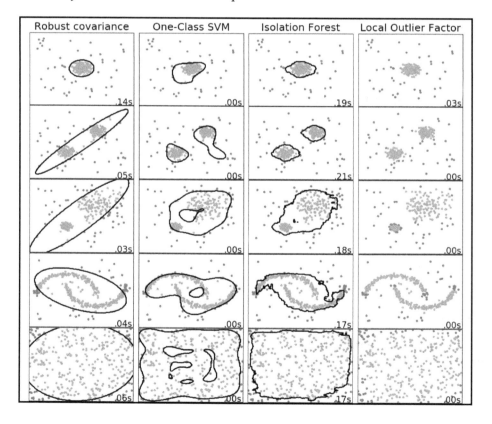

Detecting time series anomalies with Luminol

Luminol is a time series anomaly detection algorithm released by LinkedIn. It uses a bitmap to check how many detection strategies, that are robust in datasets, tend to drift. It is also very lightweight and can handle large amounts of data.

In this example, we are going to use a publicly accessible IoT dataset from the city of Chicago. The city of Chicago has IoT sensors measuring the water quality of their lakes. Because the dataset needs some massaging before we get it into the right format for anomaly detection, we will use the `prepdata.py` file to extract one data point from one lake.

Getting ready

To get ready for this recipe, you will need to download the CSV file from the GitHub repository for this book. Next, you will need to install `luminol`:

```
pip install luminol
```

How to do it...

The steps involved in this recipe are as follows:

1. Prep the data with `prepdata.py`:

```python
import pandas as pd

df = pd.read_csv('Beach_Water_Quality_-_Automated_Sensors.csv',
                  header=0)

df = df[df['Beach Name'] == 'Rainbow Beach']
df = df[df['Water Temperature'] > -100]
df = df[df['Wave Period'] > -100]
df['Measurement Timestamp'] = pd.to_datetime(df['Measurement
                                                 Timestamp'])

Turbidity = df[['Measurement Timestamp', 'Turbidity']]
Turbidity.to_csv('Turbidity.csv', index=False, header=False)
```

2. Import libraries in `Luminol.py`:

```
from luminol.anomaly_detector import AnomalyDetector
import time
```

3. Perform anomaly detection:

```
my_detector = AnomalyDetector('Turbidity.csv')
score = my_detector.get_all_scores()
```

4. Print the anomalies:

```
for (timestamp, value) in score.iteritems():
    t_str = time.strftime('%y-%m-%d %H:%M:%S',
                          time.localtime(timestamp))
    if value > 0:
        print(f'{t_str}, {value}')
```

How it works...

In the `dataprep` Python library, you will only import `pandas` so that we can take the CSV file and turn it into a `pandas` DataFrame. Once we have a `pandas` DataFrame we will filter out on `Rainbow Beach` (in our case, we are only looking at `Rainbow Beach`). Then we will take out anomalous data such as data where the water temperature is below -100 degrees. Then we will convert the `time` string into a string that pandas can read. We do this so that when it outputs, it outputs to a standard time series format. Then we select only the two columns we need to analyze, `Measurement Timestamp` and `Turbidity`. Finally, we save the file in CSV format.

Next, we create a Luminol file. From here, we use `pip` to install `luminol` and `time`. We then use the anomaly detector on the CSV file and return all of the scores. Finally, we return scores if the value of our score item is greater than 0. In other words, we only return scores if there is an anomaly.

There's more...

In addition to anomaly detection, Luminol can also form correlation analysis. This can help the analyst determine whether two time series datasets are correlated to each other. So, for example, our dataset from the city of Chicago measured various aspects of water purity in their lakes. We could compare lakes against each other to see whether there was a common effect in two different lakes at the same time.

Detecting seasonality-adjusted anomalies

Data from a temperature sensor might trend upward throughout the day if the device is outdoors. Similarly, the internal temperature of an exterior device may be lower in the winter. Not all devices are affected by seasonality but for the ones that are, choosing an algorithm that handles seasonality and trends is important. According to a research paper (*Automatic Anomaly Detection in the Cloud Via Statistical Learning*) from data scientists at Twitter, **Seasonal ESD** is a machine learning algorithm that takes seasonality and trends to find anomalies regardless of the seasonality.

For this recipe, we are going to use the city of Chicago lake water purity dataset. We are going to pull in the data file we prepared in the *Detecting time series anomalies with Luminol* recipe.

Getting ready

To get ready, you will need the Seasonal ESD library. This can be installed simply with the following `pip` command:

```
pip install sesd
```

The dataset can be found in the GitHub repository of this book.

How to do it...

The steps to execute this recipe are as follows:

1. Import the libraries:

```
import pandas as pd
import sesd
import numpy as np
```

2. Import and manipulate the data:

```
df = pd.read_csv('Beach_Water_Quality_-_Automated_Sensors.csv',
                 header=0)
df = df[df['Beach Name'] == 'Rainbow Beach']
df = df[df['Water Temperature'] > -100]
df = df[df['Wave Period'] > -100]
waveheight = df[['Wave Height']].to_numpy()
```

3. Perform anomaly detection:

```
outliers_indices = sesd.seasonal_esd(waveheight, hybrid=True,
                                      max_anomalies=2)
```

4. Output the results:

```
for idx in outliers_indices:
    print("Anomaly index: {}, anomaly value: {}"\
        .format(idx, waveheight[idx]))
```

How it works...

In this recipe, we first imported `numpy` and `pandas` for data manipulation. We then imported `sesd`, our anomaly detection package. Next, we got the raw data ready for machine learning. We did this by removing the data that clearly had an issue, such as sensors that were not working properly. We then filtered the data into one column. We then put that column through the seasonal ESD algorithm.

Similar to the Z-score algorithm in the first recipe, this recipe uses an online approach. It uses **Seasonal and Trend decomposition using Loess (STL)** decomposition as a preprocessing step before doing anomaly detection. A data source may have a trend and a season, as shown in the following graph:

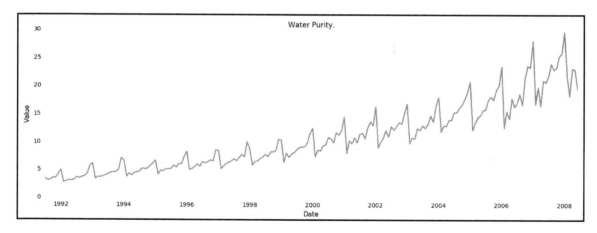

What decomposition allows you to do is look at the trend and the seasonality independently (as shown in the following trend graph). This helps to ensure the data is not affected by seasonality:

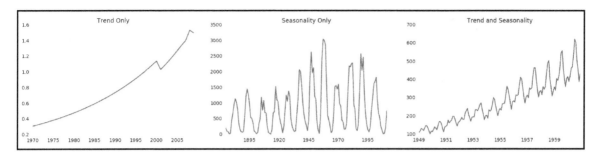

The Seasonal ESD algorithm is more complicated than the Z-score algorithm. For example, Z-score algorithms would show false positives in devices that were stationed outdoors.

Detecting spikes with streaming analytics

Stream Analytics is a tool that connects IoT Hub to other resources within Azure using a SQL interface. Stream Analytics moves data from IoT Hub to Cosmos DB, storage blobs, serverless functions, or a number of other scalable options. Streaming analytics has a few functions built-in, and you can create more functions yourself using JavaScript; anomaly detection is one of those functions. In this example, we are going to use Raspberry Pi to stream gyroscope and acceleration data to IoT Hub. Then we'll connect streaming analytics and, using its SQL interface, we will output only the anomalous results.

Getting ready

For this experiment, you will need IoT Hub. Next, you'll need to create a streaming analytics job. To do this, you will go into the Azure portal and create a new streaming analytics job through the **Create new resource** wizard. After you create a new streaming analytics job, you will see that there are three main components on the **Overview** page. These are inputs, outputs, and queries. Inputs, as the name suggests, are the streams you want to input; in our case, we are inputting IoT Hub. To connect to IoT Hub you need to click on **Inputs**, then select the input type of IoT Hub, and then select the IoT Hub instance you created for this recipe. Next, you can create an output. This could be a database such as Cosmos DB or a function app so that you can send alerts through any number of messaging systems. For the sake of simplicity, we are not going to specify output for this recipe. For testing purposes, you can review the output on the Stream Analytics query editor.

How to do it...

The steps for this recipe are as follows:

1. Import the libraries:

    ```
    #device.py

    import time
    from azure.iot.device import IoTHubDeviceClient, Message
    from sense_hat import SenseHat
    import json
    ```

2. Declare the variables:

    ```
    client = IoTHubDeviceClient.create_from_connection_string("your
    device key here")
    sense = SenseHat()
    sense.set_imu_config(True, True, True)
    ```

3. Get a joined device value:

    ```
    def combined_value(data):
        return float(data['x'])+float(data['y'])+float(data['z'])
    ```

4. Get and send the data:

    ```
    while True:
        gyro = combined_value(sense.gyro_raw)
        accel = combined_value(sense.accel_raw)
        msg_txt_formatted = msg.format(gyro=gyro, accel=accel)
        message = Message(msg_txt_formatted)
        client.send_message(message)
        time.sleep(1)
    ```

5. Create a SQL query that uses the `AnomalyDetection_SpikeAndDip` algorithm
    to detect anomalies:

    ```
    SELECT
        EVENTENQUEUEDUTCTIME AS time,
        CAST(gyro AS float) AS gyro,
        AnomalyDetection_SpikeAndDip(CAST(gyro AS float), 95, 120,
    'spikesanddips')
            OVER(LIMIT DURATION(second, 120)) AS SpikeAndDipScores
        INTO output
        FROM tempin
    ```

How it works...

To import the libraries on the Raspberry Pi you will need to log in to the Raspberry Pi and use `pip` to install `azure-iot-device` and `SenseHat`. Next, you'll need to go onto that machine and create a file called `device.py`. Then you will import the `time`, Azure IoT Hub, Sense HAT, and `json` libraries. Next, you'll need to go into IoT Hub and create a device through the portal, get your connection string, and enter it in the spot where it says **Your device key here**. You then initialize `SenseHat` and set the internal measuring units to `True`, initializing our sensors. Then create a helper function that combines our x, y, and z data. Next, get the data from sensors and send that to IoT Hub. Finally, wait for a second before sending that data again.

Next, go into the Stream Analytics job that you had set up and click on **Edit query**. From here, create a common table expression. A common table expression allows you to make a complex query more simple. Then use the built-in anomaly detection spikes and dips algorithm over a 120-second window. The quick editor allows you to test live data in the stream and view that the anomaly detectors gave the resulting score of anomalous or non-anomalous.

Detecting anomalies on the edge

In this final recipe, we are going to use `SenseHat` on the Raspberry Pi to collect data, train that data on our local computer, then deploy a machine learning model on the device. To avoid redundancy after recording your data you will need to run either of the recipes on autoencoders or isolated forest from earlier in this chapter.

People use motion sensors in IoT to ensure shipping containers are safely transported aboard ships. For example, proving that a shipping container was dropped in a particular harbor would help with insurance claims. They are also used for worker safety to detect falls or workers acting unsafely. They are also used on devices that are prone to vibration when malfunctioning. Some examples of this are washing machines, wind turbines, and cement mixers.

During the data collection phase, you will need to safely simulate falling or working unsafely. You could also put a sensor on a washing machine that is unbalanced. The data in the GitHub repository has data from normal work and data that came from dancing, which in our case we are calling **anomalous**.

Getting ready

To get ready for this you will need a Raspberry Pi with a Sense HAT. You will need a way of getting data from the Raspberry Pi. You can do this by enabling SSH or using a USB drive. On the Raspberry Pi, you will need to use pip to install sense_hat and numpy.

How to do it...

The steps for this recipe are as follows:

1. Import the libraries:

```
#Gather.py

import numpy as np
from sense_hat import SenseHat
import json
import time
```

2. Initialize the variables:

```
sense = SenseHat()
sense.set_imu_config(True, True, True)
readings = 1000
gyro,accel = sense.gyro_raw, sense.accel_raw
actions = ['normal', 'anomolous']
dat = np.array([gyro['x'], gyro['y'], gyro['z'], accel['x'],
                accel['y'], accel['z']])
x = 1
```

3. Wait for the user input to start:

```
for user_input in actions:
    activity = input('Hit enter to record '+user_input + \
                    ' activity')
```

4. Gather the data:

```
x = 1
while x < readings:
    x = x + 1
    time.sleep(0.1)
    gyro,accel = sense.gyro_raw, sense.accel_raw
    dat = np.vstack([dat, [[gyro['x'], gyro['y'], gyro['z'],
                          accel['x'], accel['y'], accel['z']]]])
    print(readings - x)
```

5. Output the files to disk for training:

```
X_test = np.concatenate((np.full(800,0), np.full(800,1)), axis=0)
y_test = np.concatenate((np.full(200,0), np.full(200,1)), axis=0)
X_train = np.concatenate((dat[0:800,:],dat[1000:1800]))
y_train = np.concatenate((dat[800:1000],dat[1800:2000]))

np.savetxt('y_train.txt', y_train,delimiter=' ', fmt="%10.8f")
np.savetxt('y_test.txt',y_test, delimiter=' ',fmt="%10.8f")
np.savetxt('X_train.txt', X_train,delimiter=' ', fmt="%10.8f")
np.savetxt('X_test.txt',X_test, delimiter=' ',fmt="%10.8f")
```

6. Copy files from the Raspberry Pi to your local computer by using a thumb drive.

7. Train an isolated forest using the isolated forest recipe and output the `pickle` file.

8. Copy the `iforrest.p` file to the Raspberry Pi and create a file called `AnomalyDetection.py`.

9. Import the libraries:

```
#AnomalyDetection.py

import numpy as np
from sense_hat import SenseHat
from pyod.models.iforest import IForest
from pyod.utils.data import generate_data
from pyod.utils.data import evaluate_print
import pickle
sense = SenseHat()
```

10. Load the machine learning file:

```
clf = pickle.load( open( "IForrest.p", "rb" ) )
```

11. Create the output for the LEDs:

```
def transform(arr):
    ret = []
    for z in arr:
        for a in z:
            ret.append(a)
    return ret

O = (10, 10, 10) # Black
X = (255, 0 ,0) # red

alert = transform([
        [X, X, O, O, O, O, X, X],
        [X, X, X, O, O, X, X, X],
        [O, X, X, X, X, X, X, O],
        [O, O, X, X, X, X, O, O],
        [O, O, X, X, X, X, O, O],
        [O, X, X, X, X, X, X, O],
        [X, X, X, O, O, X, X, X],
        [X, X, O, O, O, O, X, X]
        ])

clear = transform([
        [O, O, O, O, O, O, O, O],
        [O, O, O, O, O, O, O, O],
        [O, O, O, O, O, O, O, O],
        [O, O, O, O, O, O, O, O],
        [O, O, O, O, O, O, O, O],
        [O, O, O, O, O, O, O, O],
        [O, O, O, O, O, O, O, O],
        [O, O, O, O, O, O, O, O]
        ])
```

12. Predict the anomaly:

```
while True:
    dat = np.array([gyro['x'], gyro['y'], gyro['z'], accel['x'],
                    accel['y'], accel['z']])
    pred = clf.predict(dat)
    if pred[0] == 1:
        sense.set_pixels(alert)
    else:
        sense.set_pixels(clear)
    time.sleep(0.1)
```

How it works...

We create two files – one that gathers information (called `Gather.py`) and another that detects the anomalies on the device (called `AnomalyDetection.py`). In the `Gather.py` file, we import the classes, initialize `SenseHat`, set a variable for the number of readings we will be collecting, get both the gyroscopic and accelerometer readings, create an array of normal anonymous strings, and set the initial gyroscope and sensor ratings. Then we loop through our actions and tell the user to press *Enter* when they want to record normal greetings, and then tell them to press *Enter* when they want to record anomalous readings. From there, we gather data and give feedback to the user to let them know how many more data points they will be gathering. At this point, you should be using the device in a way that is normal for its use, such as fall detection by holding it close to your body. Then, for the next loop of anomalous readings, you drop the device. Finally, we create the training and test sets that we will use for the machine learning model. We then need to copy the data files into a local computer, and then we perform the analysis in the same way as we did the isolated forest earlier in this chapter. We would then get a `pickle` file that we will be using in the `AnomalyDetection.py` file.

From here, we need to create the `AnomalyDetection.py` file that we will be using on our Raspberry Pi. Then we load our `pickle` file, which is our machine learning model. From here, we are going to create `alert` and not-alert (`clear`) variables that we can toggle for the LED display on the sense set. Finally, we run the loop, and if it predicts that the device is acting anomalously we display an `alert` signal on the sense set; otherwise, we display a `clear` signal.

6
Computer Vision

Computer vision has come a long way in recent years. Unlike many other forms of machine learning that require complex analysis, the vast majority of computer vision problems come from simple RGB cameras. Machine learning frameworks such as Keras and OpenCV have standard and high-accuracy neural networks built-in. A few years ago, implementing a facial recognition neural net, for example, was complex and challenging to set up in Python, let alone on a high-speed device using C++ or CUDA. Today, this process is easier and more accessible than ever before. In this chapter, we are going to talk about implementing computer vision in the cloud, as well as on Edge devices such as NVIDIA Jetson Nano.

We will cover the following recipes in this chapter:

- Connecting cameras through OpenCV
- Using Microsoft's custom vision to train and label your images
- Detecting faces with deep neural nets and Caffe
- Detecting objects using YOLO on Raspberry Pi 4
- Detecting objects using GPUs on NVIDIA Jetson Nano
- Training vision with PyTorch on GPUs

Connecting cameras through OpenCV

Connecting a camera through OpenCV is fairly straightforward. The issue is often in installing OpenCV. OpenCV installs easily on a desktop computer, but on more constrained devices, it may require extra work. In a Raspberry Pi 3, for example, you may need to enable swap space. This allows the system to use the SD card as a temporary memory store. Depending on the device, there are various instructions available online on how to get OpenCV onto a challenging device.

In this recipe, we will connect OpenCV to a camera application on the Raspberry Pi Zero, but if you do not have the hardware, you can run the code on a PC. In future recipes, we will assume knowledge of this and breeze by the explanation of what is going on.

Getting ready

From a coding perspective, using OpenCV abstracts the hardware away. It does not matter if you are using a $5 Raspberry Pi Zero or a $120 LattePanda; the only things required for this recipe are a computer and a camera. Most laptops have built-in cameras, but for a desktop computer or a **single board computer** (**SBC**), such as a Raspberry Pi or LattePanda, you will need a USB web camera.

Next, you will need to install OpenCV. As mentioned earlier, there are ways of getting OpenCV on constrained devices. These are all unique to the device in question. In our case, we will put a PiCam module on a Raspberry Pi Zero. The following is an image of a PiCam module for reference:

To add the PiCam to the Pi Zero, you simply pull the black tabs from the connector, insert the PiCam module, and then push in the tab, as shown in the following image:

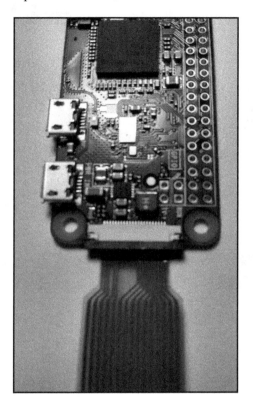

From here you need to enable the cameras in your Raspberry Pi. You will need to plug a monitor, keyboard, and mouse into your Raspberry Pi. Then, make sure that your system is up to date by executing the following commands:

```
sudo apt-get update
sudo apt-get upgrade
```

Then, you will enable the camera by going into the **Rasp Config** menu. In your terminal, type in the following:

```
sudo raspi-config
```

From there, select **Camera** and then enable it:

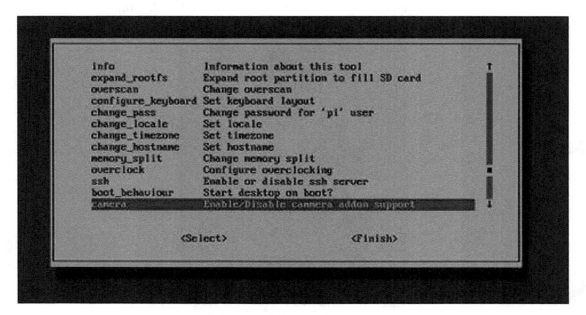

There are three different libraries that we can `pip` install: `opencv-contrib-python` for all of the OpenCV extras, `opencv-python` for a faster, but shorter, list of features, and finally `opencv-cython` for a faster Python experience.

For this book, I would recommend performing the following command:

```
pip install open-contrib-python
```

How to do it...

The steps for this recipe are as follows:

1. Import OpenCV:

```
import cv2
```

2. Select the camera:

```
cap = cv2.VideoCapture(0)
```

3. Check whether the camera is available:

```
if not (cap.isOpened()):
    print('Could not open video device')
```

4. Capture, save, and show frames from the camera:

```
x = 0
while(True):
    ret, frame = cap.read()
    cv2.imshow('preview',frame)
    time.sleep(1)
    cv2.imwrite(f'./images/cap{x}.jpg', frame)
    if cv2.waitKey(1) & 0xFF == ord('q'):
        break
```

5. Release the camera:

```
cap.release()
cv2.destroyAllWindows()
```

How it works...

In this recipe, first, we import OpenCV. We then select the first camera it finds (camera(0)). If we were looking for the second camera it finds, then we would increment the camera number (camera(1)). Next, we check whether the camera is available. There can be several reasons why a camera might not be available. First, it could be opened by something else. You could, for example, open the camera in a different application to see whether it is working and this would prevent the Python application from detecting and connecting to the camera. Another common issue is that releasing the camera step in the code does not get executed and the camera needs to be reset. Next, we capture the video frames and present them on the screen until someone presses the Q key. Finally, after someone has exited the application, we release the camera and close the open window.

There's more...

OpenCV has many tools for writing text to the screen or drawing bounding boxes around an identified object. In addition, it has the ability to downsample or change an RGB image to black and white. Filtering and downsampling are techniques that machine learning engineers perform on constrained devices that allow them to operate efficiently.

Using Microsoft's custom vision to train and label your images

Microsoft's cognitive services offer a one-stop shop for everything you need for training images and deploying models. First, it provides a way of uploading images. Then, it has a UI for drawing bounding boxes around images, and finally, it allows you to deploy and expose an API endpoint you can use for computer vision.

Getting ready

To use Microsoft's custom vision service, you will require an Azure subscription. Then you will need to spin up a new custom vision project. There is a free tier for testing out small models and a paid tier for larger models and serving models at scale. After creating the custom vision project in the Azure portal, you will see two new projects in the resource group. The first will be for training, and the second will have a -prediction label appended to the name, which will be used for the predictions.

Then you will require images of what you are classifying. In our case, we are identifying beverages in an environment with lead and carcinogen exposure. If you have completed the previous recipe, you will have a camera capturing images at 1 second intervals. To make an object detection model in cognitive services, you will need at least 30 images of each thing you are trying to classify. More images will improve accuracy. To get good accuracy, you should vary the light, background, angle, size, and type, and use individual and grouped images of the objects.

You also need to install Microsoft's cognitive services computer vision Python package. To do that, execute the following command:

```
pip3 install azure-cognitiveservices-vision-customvision
```

How to do it...

The steps for this recipe are as follows:

1. Go to the Azure portal where you created your custom vision project.

2. Navigate your browser to `https://customvision.ai` and log in with your Azure credential. This will take you to the **Projects** page. There are some sample projects, but you will want to create your own. Click on the **New project** tile. Then, fill out the **Create new project** wizard. For this recipe, we are taking pictures of food and drink items so that we can use them in a workplace safety computer vision project. This type of computer vision could be used in an electronics shop, where people are eating in an environment with contaminants such as lead or carcinogens.

3. On the main page of the project, you will see a **Tags** button. Click on the **Untagged** option (as shown in the following screenshot) and you will see all of the images that you uploaded:

4. Click on the image and use the tools to draw a bounding box around the images. From here, you can draw bounding boxes around your images and tag them:

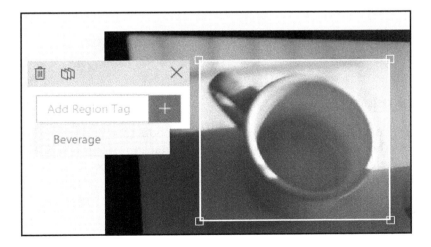

5. Next, click on the green **Train** button to train the model:

6. After you click on **Train**, it will start to train a model. This could take quite some time. Once it completes, click on the iteration and then click on the **Prediction URL** button:

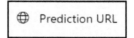

This will give you a window with everything you require in order to send an image to the object detection service.

The code for testing the model is as follows:

```
import requests
file = open('images/drink1/cap0.jpg', 'rb')
url = 'Your iteration url goes here'
headers = {'Prediction-Key': 'key from the prediction url', \
           'Content-Type':'application/octet-stream'}
files = {'file': file}
r = requests.post(url, data=file, headers=headers)
json_data = r.json()
print(json_data)
```

How it works...

Cognitive services use the tagged images to create a model that finds those images within a larger picture. As the number of images increases, so does the accuracy. There will be a point where, however, when the accuracy reaches convergence or, in layman's terms, does not improve. To find this convergence, add and tag more images until the iteration metrics of **Precision**, **Recall**, and **mAP** do not improve. The custom vision dashboard in the following screenshot shows the three factors that we measure to show the model's accuracy:

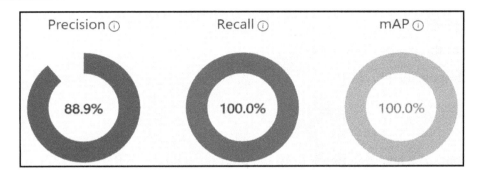

Detecting faces with deep neural nets and Caffe

One advantage of using OpenCV's implementation of visual neural networks is that they are available on different platforms. For the sake of clarity and brevity, we are using Python on an environment that has Python installed. However, the same results could be used with OpenCV's C++ implementation on an ARM-CortexM3 or OpenCV's Java implementation on an Android system. In this recipe, we are going to use a face detection neural network that OpenCV implemented based on the **Caffe** machine learning framework. The output of this recipe will be a window on the PC that has the image with bounding boxes around the face.

Getting ready

To run this recipe, you will need a web camera attached to your device. You will need to install OpenCV, NumPy, and Imutils, if you have already not done so. Installing OpenCV can be challenging on very constrained devices. There are several ways in which you can attempt to do this if you are unable to install it natively on a device. Many devices with extra storage space will allow you to use the disk as swap space for the memory. If the device in question supports dockerization, then you can compile on a computer and run the container on the device. This recipe uses a pretrained model that can be found in the GitHub companion to this book in the Ch6 directory.

How to do it...

The steps for this recipe are as follows:

1. Import the libraries:

```
import cv2
import numpy as np
import imutils
```

2. Import a neural network from the pretrained model in the Ch6 GitHub repo and then initialize OpenCV's camera operator:

```
net = cv2.dnn.readNetFromCaffe("deploy.prototxt.txt",
"res10_300x300_ssd_iter_140000.caffemodel")
cap = cv2.VideoCapture(0)
```

3. Create a function that downsamples the image and transforms it into a predefined shape for our neural network and then perform the inference:

```
def FaceNN(frame):
    frame = imutils.resize(frame, width=300, height=300)
    (h, w) = frame.shape[:2]
    blob = cv2.dnn.blobFromImage(frame, 1.0, (300, 300),
                                 (103.93, 116.77, 123.68))
    net.setInput(blob)
    detections = net.forward()
```

4. Draw the bounding boxes:

```
for i in range(0, detections.shape[2]):
    confidence = detections[0, 0, i, 2]
    if confidence < .8:
        continue
    box = detections[0, 0, i, 3:7] * np.array([w, h, w, h])
    (startX, startY, endX, endY) = box.astype("int")
    text = "{:.2f}%".format(confidence * 100)
    y = startY - 10 if startY - 10 > 10 else startY + 10
    cv2.rectangle(frame, (startX, startY), (endX, endY),
                  (0, 0, 300), 2)
    cv2.putText(frame, text, (startX, y), cv2.FONT_HERSHEY_SIMPLEX,
                0.45, (0, 0, 300), 2)
```

5. Return the image with bounding boxes:

```
return frame
```

6. Create a never-ending loop that reads an image from the camera, performs the inference and gets the overlay, and then outputs the image to the screen:

```
while True:
    ret, frame = cap.read()
    image = FaceNN(frame)
    cv2.imshow('frame',image)
    if cv2.waitKey(1) & 0xFF == ord('q'):
        break
```

7. Finally, clean up and destroy all the windows:

```
cap.release()
cv2.destroyAllWindows()
```

How it works...

After importing our libraries, we import the pretrained face detection model into our `net` variable. We then open the first camera (0). Then we use `FacNN` to predict the image and draw the bounding box. Then we shrink the image to an appropriate dimension. We then use `imutils` to resize our large image from the camera. We then set the image in the network and get the face detections. Next, we get the face detections and retrieve the confidence that the object it finds is really a face. In our case, we are using a `.8` or `80%` threshold. We also filter out faces with low confidence. We then draw bounding boxes around the faces and put confidence text on the boxes. We then return those images to our main `while True` loop and display them on the screen. We also wait for a *Q* key to quit. Finally, we release the camera and destroy the UI window.

Detecting objects using YOLO on Raspberry Pi 4

YOLO stands for **you only look once**. It is a fast image classification library that is optimized for GPU processing. YOLO tends to outperform all other computer vision libraries. In this recipe, we are going to implement a computer vision object detection using OpenCV's implementation of YOLO. In this example, we are going to use a pretrained model that has 40 common objects already trained.

Getting ready

To get ready, you will need to clone the GitHub repo for this book. In the Ch6 section, you will find the yolov3.cfg config file and the yolov3.txt text file of the classes. Next, you will need to download the large weights file. To do this, you will need to open a command prompt and cd into the Ch6 directory and then download the weights file with the following command:

```
wget https://pjreddie.com/media/files/yolov3.weights
```

Additionally, you will need to install OpenCV and NumPy.

How to do it...

The steps for this recipe are as follows:

1. Import the libraries:

```
import cv2
import numpy as np
```

2. Set the variables:

```
with open("yolov3.txt", 'r') as f:
    classes = [line.strip() for line in f.readlines()]
colors = np.random.uniform(0, 300, size=(len(classes), 3))
net = cv2.dnn.readNet("yolov3.weights", "yolov3.cfg")
cap = cv2.VideoCapture(0)
scale = 0.00392
conf_threshold = 0.5
nms_threshold = 0.4
```

3. Define our output layers:

```
def get_output_layers(net):
    layer_names = net.getLayerNames()
    output_layers = [layer_names[i[0] - 1] for i in \
                     net.getUnconnectedOutLayers()]
    return output_layers
```

4. Create bounding boxes:

```
def create_bounding_boxes(outs,Width, Height):
    boxes = []
    class_ids = []
    confidences = []
    for out in outs:
        for detection in out:
            scores = detection[5:]
            class_id = np.argmax(scores)
            confidence = scores[class_id]
            if confidence > conf_threshold:
                center_x = int(detection[0] * Width)
                center_y = int(detection[1] * Height)
                w = int(detection[2] * Width)
                h = int(detection[3] * Height)
                x = center_x - w / 2
                y = center_y - h / 2
                class_ids.append(class_id)
                confidences.append(float(confidence))
                boxes.append([x, y, w, h])
    return boxes, class_ids, confidences
```

5. Draw bounding boxes:

```
def draw_bounding_boxes(img, class_id, confidence, box):
    x = round(box[0])
    y = round(box[1])
    w = round(box[2])
    h =round(box[3])
    x_plus_w = x+w
    y_plus_h = y+h
    label = str(classes[class_id])
    color = colors[class_id]
    cv2.rectangle(img, (x,y), (x_plus_w,y_plus_h), color, 2)
    cv2.putText(img, label, (x-10,y-10), cv2.FONT_HERSHEY_SIMPLEX,
                0.5, color, 2)
```

6. Process the images:

```
def Yolo(image):
    try:
        Width = image.shape[1]
        Height = image.shape[0]
        blob = cv2.dnn.blobFromImage(image, scale, (416,416),
                                     (0,0,0), True, crop=False)
        net.setInput(blob)
        outs = net.forward(get_output_layers(net))
```

```
        boxes, class_ids, confidences = \
            create_bounding_boxes(outs, Width, Height)
        indices = cv2.dnn.NMSBoxes(boxes, confidences,
                                   conf_threshold, nms_threshold)

        for i in indices:
            i = i[0]
            box = boxes[i]

            draw_bounding_boxes(image, class_ids[i],
                                confidences[i], box)
    except Exception as e:
        print('Failed dnn: '+ str(e))

    return image
```

7. Read the camera:

```
while True:
    ret, frame = cap.read()
    image = Yolo(frame)
    cv2.imshow('frame',image)
    if cv2.waitKey(1) & 0xFF == ord('q'):
        break
```

8. Finally, clean up and destroy all the windows:

```
cap.release()
cv2.destroyAllWindows()
```

How it works...

YOLO looks at the image once and divides the image up into a grid. It then uses bounding boxes to divide up the grid. YOLO first determines whether the bounding box has an object and then determines the class of object. By incorporating a prefilter on the algorithm, this screens out parts of the images that are not objects and YOLO is then able to dramatically speed up its search.

In this example, after importing our libraries, we set our variables. First, we open `yolov3.txt`. This file contains the classes of the pretrained library we will be using. Next, we create a random `color` array to denote our different objects as different colors. Then we import our libraries and set our camera to the first camera on the computer. We then set thresholds and scale images so that the image sizes are something that would be recognizable to the classifier. If we, for example, add a high-resolution image, the classifier might only recognize very small things as objects while ignoring larger things. This is because YOLO tries to determine bounding boxes around objects to filter out things that are objects. Next, we define our output layers and then create bounding boxes based on our confidence threshold. We then use these bounding boxes to draw rectangles around the images and passed that image in addition to the labeled text back to our image processor. Our main image processing loop calls the `Yolo` function. Finally, before cleaning up our resources, we run through the main loop that performs YOLO analysis.

Detecting objects using GPUs on NVIDIA Jetson Nano

NVIDIA makes a series of GPU-enabled SBCs. Some of these, such as the TX2, are used on drones because they are lightweight and can pack a lot of power under their GPU-enabled systems. GPUs, along with **Tensor Processing Units** (**TPUs**), are able to deliver multiple times the computer vision capabilities compared with standard CPUs. In this recipe, we will use NVIDIA Jetson Nano, which is their least expensive development board at $99. The Jetson has an ecosystem of libraries that only work on their products.

Getting ready

First, you will need an NVIDIA Jetson. Then you will need to install the operating system. To do this, you will need to flash a micro USB with NVIDIA's Jetpack image. The Jetpack image consists of a base Ubuntu image with many of the dev tools you will need in order to get going. Once you have your OS image, put it into the Jetson with a monitor, keyboard, mouse, and network-attached.

Then you will update the OS, as follows:

```
sudo apt-get update
```

After that, you will need to install the extra software to run the code:

```
sudo apt-get install git
sudo apt-get install cmake
sudo apt-get install libpython3-dev
sudo apt-get install python3-numpygpu sbc
```

Once you have done that, you will need to download the starter project from Jetson:

```
git clone --recursive https://github.com/dusty-nv/jetson-inference
```

Then you will make and navigate to the `build` directory:

```
cd jetson-inference
mkdir build
cd build
```

From here we will make, install, and link the code from the repository:

```
cmake ../
make
sudo make install
sudo ldconfig
```

After running `make`, you will get a dialog in your terminal offering you the ability to download some different pretrained models and also PyTorch so that you can train your own models. Use the wizard to first select the models you want to download:

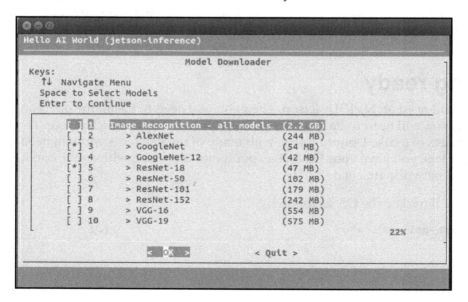

The tool will download all the models you selected:

```
[jetson-inference]  Downloading ResNet-50...
ResNet-50.tar.gz    100%[===================>]  91.09M  1.69MB/s    in 52s
[jetson-inference]  Downloading SSD-Mobilenet-v2...
SSD-Mobilenet-v2.ta 100%[===================>]  59.61M  22.1MB/s    in 2.7s
[jetson-inference]  Downloading SSD-Inception-v2...
SSD-Inception-v2.ta 100%[===================>]  88.25M  26.6MB/s    in 3.8s
[jetson-inference]  Downloading PedNet...
ped-100.tar.gz      100%[===================>]  21.99M  14.3MB/s    in 1.5s
```

For this recipe, you can keep the default models. After selecting **OK**, it will ask you to install PyTorch so that you can train your own models. Select **PyTorch** and then select **OK**.

How to do it...

The steps for this recipe are as follows:

1. Import the Jetson libraries:

    ```
    import jetson.inference
    import jetson.utils
    ```

2. Set the variables:

    ```
    net = jetson.inference.detectNet("ssd-inception-v2", threshold=0.5)
    camera = jetson.utils.gstCamera(1280,720,"/dev/video0")
    display = jetson.utils.glDisplay()
    ```

3. Then, run the camera display loop:

    ```
    while display.IsOpen():
        img, width, height = camera.CaptureRGBA()
        detections = net.Detect(img,width, height)
        display.RenderOnce(img,width,height)
    ```

How it works...

In this recipe, we added the libraries and then we cloned the Jetson inference repository. We then ran a series of make and linker tools to get the install working correctly. During this process, we downloaded a large set of pretrained models. We then started writing our code. Because the Jetson is limited in terms of its capabilities and memory, installing a full-featured IDE can be wasteful. One workaround for this is to use an IDE that supports SSH, such as Visual Studio Code, and remoting into the box via the IDE. You can then work with the device without tying up resources on the Jetson Nano.

To build out this project, first, we import the Jetson inference and `utils` libraries. In the previous recipes, we did a lot of the low-level work ourselves as far as using OpenCV to get the camera and then used other libraries to manipulate the images and draw bounding boxes. With Jetson's libraries, the vast majority of that code is handled for you. After we imported the libraries, we imported the models we downloaded earlier and set a threshold. Then we entered it in the camera dimensions and set the camera to `/dev/video0`. Next, we set our visual display. Finally, we grabbed the camera image, ran the detection algorithm, and then output that camera image to the screen with the bounding boxes.

There's more...

As we mentioned earlier, NVIDIA has an ecosystem for their products. They have helpful containers, models, and tutorials to work efficiently with their hardware. To aid you, they have a product website that gets you started with training models and building out containerized notebooks. They have dozens of prebuilt containers for different libraries, including PyTorch and TensorFlow to name a few. They also have dozens of pretrained models using everything from pose detection to specific industry models. They even have their own cloud where you can train your models if you wish. You can, however, run locally as well. Their website is `https://ngc.nvidia.com/`.

Training vision with PyTorch on GPUs

In the previous recipe, we implemented an object classifier using GPU and an NVIDIA Jetson Nano. There are other types of GPU-enabled devices. These range from the NVIDIA TX2, which can be put on a drone to do real-time analysis of pipelines, to industrial PCs running GPUs and using computer vision to perform analyses on workplace safety. In this recipe, we are going to train and add to an existing image classification model by adding our own images to it.

Challenges that the IoT faces include **over-the-air** (**OTA**) updates and fleet management. IoT Edge is a conceptual framework that solves this. In OTA updates, Docker containers are used as an update mechanism. The underlying systems can be updated without having to worry about complete device failure. If an update does not work, the system can be rolled back because container failures do not affect the main OS and the Docker daemon can perform the update and roll back.

In this recipe, we are going to use NVIDIA Docker containers to build our models. Later, we will use that model for inference.

Getting ready

To get ready, we are going to use Docker with an application version greater than 19. In Docker 19, the `--gpu` tag was added, allowing you to use Docker to access the GPU natively. Depending on your GPUs, you may need to install additional drivers to make the GPUs work on your machine.

We are also going to be using **Visual Studio Code** (**VS Code**), which, with the help of a plugin, allows you to write code directly in NVIDIA's GPU PyTorch container. You will need to perform the following steps:

1. Download and install VS Code and then use the extension manager to add the **Remote Development Extension Pack** by clicking on the extension icon.
2. Optionally, you can sign up for NVIDIA GPU Cloud, which has a catalog of containers and models.
3. Pull the NVIDIA Docker image for PyTorch:

   ```
   docker pull nvcr.io/nvidia/pytorch:20.02-py3
   ```

4. Create a folder where you want to map the code to on your computer. Then, in a terminal window, navigate to the directory you created.
5. Run the Docker container:

   ```
   docker run --gpus all -it --rm -v $(pwd):/data/
   nvcr.io/nvidia/pytorch:20.02-py3
   ```

6. Open VS Code and connect to your container by clicking on the ▨ button and then, in the dialog box, enter `Remote-Containers: Attach to a running container`. This will give you a list of the running containers. Then, open the `/data` folder.

7. Put your images in a data folder with the folder labeled as the class name. There is an example of this, complete with images, in the GitHub repo for this recipe.

8. Test the container to make sure that the container is up and running and that all of the drivers are installed. In the terminal window that you started the container with, type in `python` and then execute the following code:

```python
import torch
print(torch.cuda.is_available())
```

If it returns `True`, you are ready to train with GPUs. If not, you may need to troubleshoot your environment.

How to do it...

The steps for this recipe are as follows:

1. Import the libraries:

```python
import numpy as np
import torch
from torch import nn
from torch import optim
import torch.nn.functional as F
from torchvision import datasets, transforms, models
from torch.utils.data.sampler import SubsetRandomSampler
```

2. Declare your variables:

```python
datadir = './data/train'
valid_size = .3
epochs = 3
steps = 0
running_loss = 0
print_every = 10
train_losses = []
test_losses = []
```

3. Make an accuracy printer:

```
def print_score(torch, testloader, inputs, device, model,
criterion, labels):
test_loss = 0
accuracy = 0
model.eval()daimen

with torch.no_grad():
    for inputs, labels in testloader:
        inputs, labels = inputs.to(device), labels.to(device)
        logps = model.forward(inputs)
        batch_loss = criterion(logps, labels)
        test_loss += batch_loss.item()

        ps = torch.exp(logps)
        top_p, top_class = ps.topk(1, dim=1)
        equals = top_class == labels.view(*top_class.shape)
        accuracy +=
torch.mean(equals.type(torch.FloatTensor)).item()

train_losses.append(running_loss/len(trainloader))
test_losses.append(test_loss/len(testloader))
print(f"Epoch {epoch+1}/{epochs} \
        Train loss: {running_loss/print_every:.3f} \
        Test loss: {test_loss/len(testloader):.3f} \
        Test accuracy: {accuracy/len(testloader):.3f}")

 return test_loss, accuracy
```

4. Import the images:

```
train_transforms = transforms.Compose([transforms.Resize(224),
                                    transforms.ToTensor()])
test_transforms = transforms.Compose([transforms.Resize(224),
                                    transforms.ToTensor()])
train_data = datasets.ImageFolder(datadir,
                            transform=train_transforms)
test_data = datasets.ImageFolder(datadir,
                            transform=test_transforms)
num_train = len(train_data)
indices = list(range(num_train))
split = int(np.floor(valid_size * num_train))
np.random.shuffle(indices)
train_idx, test_idx = indices[split:], indices[:split]
train_sampler = SubsetRandomSampler(train_idx)
test_sampler = SubsetRandomSampler(test_idx)
trainloader = torch.utils.data.DataLoader(train_data,
```

```
                                    sampler=train_sampler,
                                    batch_size=1)
testloader = torch.utils.data.DataLoader(test_data,
                                    sampler=test_sampler,
                                    batch_size=1)
```

5. Set up the network:

```
device = torch.device("cuda" if torch.cuda.is_available() else
"cpu")
model = models.resnet50(pretrained=True)

for param in model.parameters():
    param.requires_grad = False

model.fc = nn.Sequential(nn.Linear(2048, 512), nn.ReLU(),
                        nn.Dropout(0.2), nn.Linear(512, 10),
                        nn.LogSoftmax(dim=1))
criterion = nn.NLLLoss()
optimizer = optim.Adam(model.fc.parameters(), lr=0.003)
model.to(device)
```

6. Train the model:

```
for epoch in range(epochs):
    for inputs, labels in trainloader:
        steps += 1
        inputs, labels = inputs.to(device), labels.to(device)
        optimizer.zero_grad()
        logps = model.forward(inputs)
        loss = criterion(logps, labels)
        loss.backward()
        optimizer.step()
        running_loss += loss.item()

        if steps % print_every == 0:
            test_loss, accuracy = print_score(torch, testloader,
                                        inputs, device,
                                        model, criterion,
                                        labels)

            running_loss = 0
            model.train()
```

7. Save your model:

```
torch.save(model, 'saftey.pth')
```

How it works...

In this recipe, we used a Docker container from NVIDIA to bypass the many steps it requires to install NVIDIA GPU on a local computer. We used VS Code to connect to the running Docker container and we tested it to make sure the container was capable of using the GPUs. We then developed our code.

First, as always, we imported our libraries. Then we declared our variables. The first variable is the location of the training data, the split amount, the number of epochs, and the steps run. We then made a function that prints the results on screen so that we could see whether our model was improving with changes to the hyperparameters. We then imported the images from our training folder. After that, we set up our neural network. Next, we imported the ResNet 50 model. We set the model's `requires_grad` parameters to `false` so that our code would not affect the already existing model. We are using a sequential linear neural network using ReLU for our activation function with a dropout of 20%. We then added a smaller network as our output layer using softmax as our activation function. We use `Adam` to perform stochastic optimization. We then ran it through our epochs and trained the model. Finally, the model was saved.

There's more...

You may want to test your newly trained image classifier. There is an inference tester in the GitHub repo for this book under `Ch6 -> pyImage -> inferance.py`. In the NVIDIA developer portal, you will find everything you need, from how to manage GPU usage effectively across a Kubernetes cluster to information on how to deploy the model you just created on a device for a drone such as a TX2.

7
NLP and Bots for Self-Ordering Kiosks

Language understanding has improved dramatically over the past few years. New algorithms and hardware have come out that have dramatically changed the effectiveness of the feasibility of voice-activated systems. In addition, the ability for computers to accurately sound like a human has achieved near perfection. Another area where machine learning has made large strides in the past few years is **natural language processing** (**NLP**), or as some would call it, language understanding.

When you combine computer voice with language understanding, then new markets open up for voice-activated technologies such as smart kiosks and smart devices.

We will cover the following recipes in this chapter:

- Wake word detection
- Speech-to-text using Microsoft Speech API
- Getting started with LUIS
- Implementing smart bots
- Creating a custom voice
- Enhancing bots with QnA Maker

Wake word detection

Wake word detection is used to make sure that your voice-activated system does not behave in unexpected ways. Achieving high accuracy rates for audio is challenging. Background noises interfere with the main vocal commands. One way to achieve higher accuracy is to use an array microphone. Array microphones are used for background noise canceling. In this recipe, we are using the ROOBO array microphone and the Microsoft Speech Devices SDK. The ROOBO array microphone is ideal for voice kiosks because its form factor allows it to be put flat on a kiosk face.

The ROOBO has an Android-based compute module attached to it. Android is a very common platform for kiosks because it is inexpensive and has a touch-first interface. For this recipe, we will be using the Android version of the Microsoft Speech Devices SDK. The Speech Devices SDK is different from the Speech SDK. The Speech Devices SDK will work with both array and circular microphones, while the Speech SDK is for using a single microphone. The following is a photo of a ROOBO array microphone:

Getting ready

For this recipe, you are going to need an Azure subscription and a ROOBO linear array or circular microphone. On your PC, you will also need to download and install Android Studio and **Vysor** for working with the ROOBO. To set up the device, take the following steps:

1. Download and install Android Studio.
2. Download and install Vysor.
3. Power on the device and connect it to your computer. There are two USB connectors: one labeled power and one labeled debug. Connect the power connector to a power source and the debug USB cable to your computer:

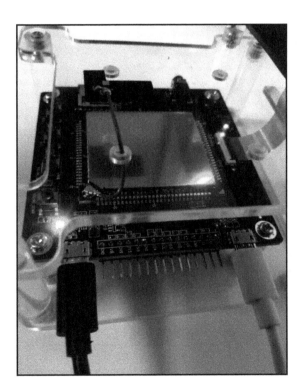

4. Open Vysor and select the device to view:

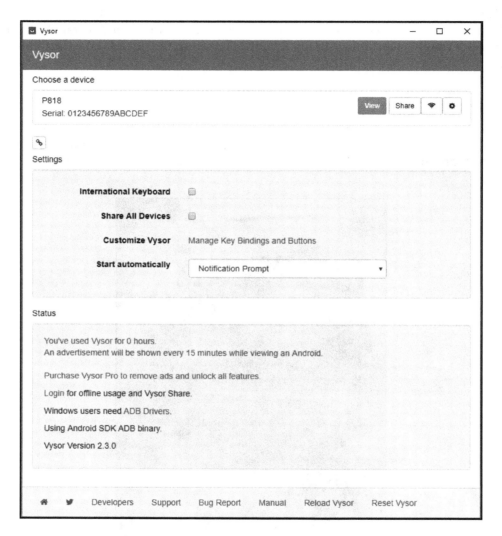

5. Click on **Settings**:

Now that we have completed the device setup, let us generate a wake word. To generate a wake word, take the following steps:

1. Go to `https://speech.microsoft.com/` and click on **Get started**:

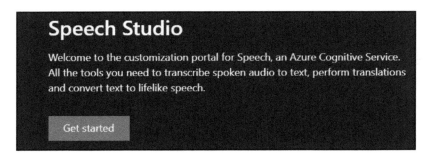

2. Select **New Project** and fill out the custom speech form, and then click **Create**:

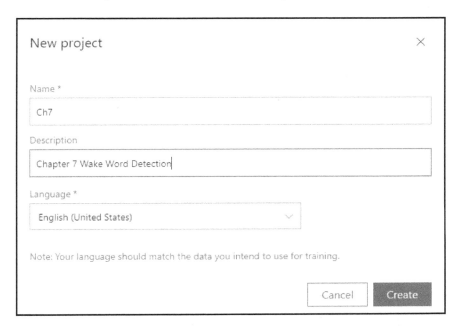

3. Click on **Create Model**.
4. Fill in the form with the wake word you wish to train. Then, click **Next**:

5. Listen to and approve the pronunciations, then click **Train**:

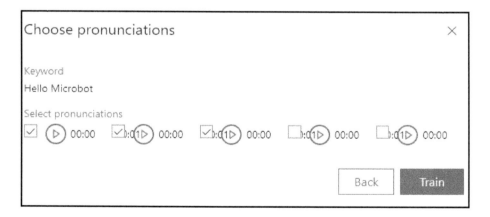

6. The model will take 20 minutes to train. When it is done, click **Download**.

How to do it...

The steps for this recipe are as follows:

1. In Android Studio, create a new project using Java:

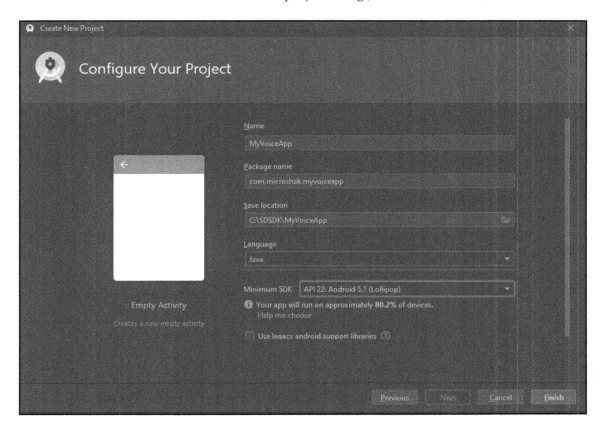

2. In the **Gradle scripts** section, change the `Gradle Voice Projects` folder and add the reference to the library:

```
allprojects {
    repositories {
        google()
        jcenter()
        mavenCentral()
        maven {
            url
'https://csspeechstorage.blob.core.windows.net/maven/'
        }
    }
}
```

3. In the **Gradle scripts** section, in the **Gradle build app** section, add this line to the dependencies section:

```
implementation 'com.microsoft.cognitiveservices.speech:client-
sdk:1.10.0'
```

4. Import the libraries needed for this project:

```
import androidx.appcompat.app.AppCompatActivity;
import
com.microsoft.cognitiveservices.speech.KeywordRecognitionModel;
import com.microsoft.cognitiveservices.speech.SpeechConfig;
import com.microsoft.cognitiveservices.speech.SpeechRecognizer;
import com.microsoft.cognitiveservices.speech.audio.AudioConfig;

import java.io.IOException;
import java.util.ArrayList;
import java.util.concurrent.ExecutorService;
import java.util.concurrent.Future;

import android.content.res.AssetManager;
import android.os.Bundle;
import android.text.Layout;
import android.text.TextUtils;
import android.view.View;
import android.widget.Button;
import android.widget.TextView;
```

5. In the main activity class, add the keys and location of the trained model. Also, add the microphone type; in this case, we are using a linear microphone:

```
public class MainActivity extends AppCompatActivity {
    private static String SpeechSubscriptionKey = "Your key here";
```

```
private static String SpeechRegion = "westus2";
//your location here

private TextView recognizedTextView;
private static String LanguageRecognition = "en-US";
private Button recognizeKwsButton;


private static String Keyword = "computer";
private static String KeywordModel = "computer.zip";

private static String DeviceGeometry = "Linear4";
private static String SelectedGeometry = "Linear4";
protected static ExecutorService s_executorService;

final AssetManager assets = this.getAssets();
```

6. Create the method that will display the result to the UI:

```
private void setTextbox(final String s) {
    MainActivity.this.runOnUiThread(() -> {
        recognizedTextView.setText(s);
        final Layout layout = recognizedTextView.getLayout();
        if (layout != null) {
            int scrollDelta = layout.getLineBottom(
                recognizedTextView.getLineCount() - 1)
                    - recognizedTextView.getScrollY() -
                recognizedTextView.getHeight();
            if (scrollDelta > 0) {
                recognizedTextView.scrollBy(0, scrollDelta);
            }
        }
    });
}
```

7. Set audio input by using the default microphone:

```
private AudioConfig getAudioConfig() {
    return AudioConfig.fromDefaultMicrophoneInput();
}
```

8. Set the task listener for the on-complete event:

```
private interface OnTaskCompletedListener<T> {
    void onCompleted(T taskResult);
}
```

9. Configure the speech settings, such as device geometry, speech region, and language:

```
public static SpeechConfig getSpeechConfig() {
    SpeechConfig speechConfig = SpeechConfig.fromSubscription(
        SpeechSubscriptionKey, SpeechRegion);

    speechConfig.setProperty("DeviceGeometry", DeviceGeometry);
    speechConfig.setProperty("SelectedGeometry",
                        SelectedGeometry);
    speechConfig.setSpeechRecognitionLanguage(
        LanguageRecognition);

    return speechConfig;
}
```

10. Set an on-complete task listener:

```
private <T> void setOnTaskCompletedListener(Future<T> task,
    OnTaskCompletedListener<T> listener) {
        s_executorService.submit(() -> {
            T result = task.get();
            listener.onCompleted(result);
            return null;
        });
    }
```

11. Set on-click buttons and a keyword listener:

```
@Override
    protected void onCreate(Bundle savedInstanceState) {
        super.onCreate(savedInstanceState);
        setContentView(R.layout.activity_main);

        recognizeKwsButton =
        findViewById(R.id.buttonRecognizeKws);
        recognizedTextView = findViewById(R.id.recognizedText);

        recognizeKwsButton.setOnClickListener(new
        View.OnClickListener() {
            private static final String delimiter = "\n";
            private final ArrayList<String> content = new
            ArrayList<>();
            private SpeechRecognizer reco = null;

            @Override
            public void onClick(View view) {
                content.clear();
```

```
                      content.add("");
                      content.add("");
                      try {
                          final KeywordRecognitionModel
                          keywordRecognitionModel =
                          KeywordRecognitionModel.fromStream(
                          assets.open(KeywordModel),Keyword,true);

                          final Future<Void> task =
                          reco.startKeywordRecognitionAsync(
                              keywordRecognitionModel);
                          setOnTaskCompletedListener(task,result ->{
                              content.set(0, "say `" + Keyword +
                                          "`...");
                              setTextbox(TextUtils.join(delimiter,
                              content));
                          });

                      } catch (IOException e) {
                          e.printStackTrace();
                      }
                  }});
              }
          }
```

How it works...

The Microsoft Speech Devices SDK is designed to work with linear and circular microphone arrays. In this recipe, we created an Android application to give the user a UI associated with the voice. Android's touch-first interface is a common form factor for kiosks. We also created a wake word file in Azure's Speech Studio. We then retrieved the keys from our service.

There's more...

The Speech Devices SDK does more than create a wake word. It does speech recognition, language understanding, and translation. If your kiosk is going to be put in a place with background noise that could interfere with the main subject of your voice recognition, then an array microphone will be your best option.

At the beginning of this recipe, we mentioned that the Speech Devices SDK also supports circular microphones. While array microphones are designed to point directly at the person talking, circular microphones are designed to be put perpendicular to the people talking. They can help determine the direction of the person speaking and are often used in a multi-speaker scenario, such as diarization.

Speech-to-text using the Microsoft Speech API

Microsoft Speech Services is an ecosystem of speech-to-text, text-to-speech, and translation features, among others. It supports multiple languages and has advanced features such as customizing the speech recognition to support accents, proper names (such as product names), background noise, and microphone quality. In this recipe, we will implement the Microsoft Speech SDK using Python.

Getting ready

First, you will need to go into the Azure portal and create a speech service. You will then go to the **Quick start** section and copy down the key.

Then, install the Azure Speech SDK:

```
python -m pip install azure-cognitiveservices-speech
```

How to do it...

The steps for this recipe are as follows:

1. Import the libraries:

   ```
   import azure.cognitiveservices.speech as speechsdk
   import time
   ```

2. Import the key that was generated in the *Getting ready* section:

   ```
   speech_key, service_region = "Your Key", "westus2"
   ```

3. Initialize the speech service:

```
speech_config = speechsdk.SpeechConfig(subscription=speech_key,
                                       region=service_region)
speech_recognizer = \
speechsdk.SpeechRecognizer(speech_config=speech_config)
speech_recognizer.session_started.connect(lambda evt: \
    print('SESSION STARTED: {}'.format(evt)))
speech_recognizer.session_stopped.connect(lambda evt: \
    print('\nSESSION STOPPED {}'.format(evt)))
speech_recognizer.recognized.connect(lambda evt: \
    print('\n{}'.format(evt.result.text)))
```

4. Then, perform continuous speech recognition by using an infinite loop:

```
try:
    while True:
        speech_recognizer.start_continuous_recognition()
        time.sleep(10)
        speech_recognizer.stop_continuous_recognition()
```

5. Finally, clean up and disconnect the session:

```
except KeyboardInterrupt:
    speech_recognizer.session_started.disconnect_all()
    speech_recognizer.recognized.disconnect_all()
    speech_recognizer.session_stopped.disconnect_all()
```

How it works...

Cognitive Services takes individual words and uses machine learning to piece them together into meaningful sentences. The SDK takes care of finding the microphone, sending the audio to Cognitive Services, and returning the results.

In the next recipe, we are going to use language understanding to determine the meaning of the speech. After that, we are going to make a smart bot using Bot Framework, which builds upon the language understanding to give state and logic to the ordering kiosk. You can use speech as an input to that system.

The Microsoft Speech SDK allows you to account for accents, pronunciations, and sound quality through its custom speech service. You can also use Docker containers for environments with limited connectivity to the internet.

Getting started with LUIS

Language Understanding, or **LUIS**, from Microsoft, is a service that takes text and extracts out of the text the entities, the things the sentence was about, the intents, and the actions of a sentence. Because having a narrow-focused domain helps reduce the error rate, the LUIS authorizing service helps users to create a pre-defined list of entities and intents for LUIS to parse.

Getting ready

LUIS is a product of Azure's Cognitive Services. You will need to log in to the Azure portal and create a LUIS resource. Then, go to `https://preview.luis.ai` and click on **New App for Conversation**. Then, fill out the form for the name, language, and prediction resource you set up.

Then, click on **Entities** in the side menu and add, as in our restaurant ordering kiosk, `Cheese burger`, `French Fries`, `Diet Pepsi`, `Milk Shake`, `Chocolate`, `Vanilla`, and so on:

Entities ?

+ Create   + Add prebuilt entity   + Add prebuilt domain entity

Name ↑	Type
Chocolate	ML
Diet Pepsi	ML
French Fries	ML
Milk Shake	ML
Vanilla	ML
Cheese burger	ML

Once you have enough entities added, you will need to add intents. Click on the intents, then add an intent. In our recipe, we are going to add a `Menu.Add item` intent. Then, we add some example sentences of how someone would order at a kiosk. We then click on the entities in the sentences and tag them:

When there is enough to represent the entire menu, click on the **Train** button at the upper right of the window. After it has completed training, click on the **Publish** button. After the publishing is completed, a notification will appear on the screen giving you the keys, endpoints, and a sample query you can put in your browser's URL bar to get a prediction.

Then, create a new intent for other actions someone would take in an ordering kiosk, such as removing items from an order or changing orders. Copy that query string because we are going to use it later.

How to do it...

The steps for this recipe are as follows:

1. Import the `requests` library to allow us to use a web service:

   ```
   import requests
   ```

2. Enter your order text:

   ```
   text_query = "give me a vanilla milk shake"
   ```

3. Send a message to LUIS:

```
r = requests.get(f'Your Copied URL String={text_query}')
```

4. Get the intents and entities from the response:

```
message = r.json()
print(message['prediction']['topIntent'])
for entity in message['prediction']['entities']['$instance']:
    print(entity)
```

How it works...

LUIS is a system that breaks down sentences and extracts their objects (entities) and actions (intents). In our recipe, we created a set of entities and intents. LUIS is able to extract these entities and intents from sentences even if they are similar to the sample phrases we typed in but not exactly the same. For example, the phrase *A vanilla shake would be lovely* is not something that we trained our model on and yet LUIS is still able to understand that this is an order for a vanilla milkshake.

There's more...

Sending text to LUIS and getting a JSON payload back is the tip of the iceberg for LUIS. LUIS is integrated with the Microsoft Speech SDK, meaning you can get entities and intents from using a microphone. You can use on-board speech recognition with devices such as smartphones and send just the text to LUIS. As is our *Wake word detection* recipe, you can use an array microphone to filter background noise or understand the directionality of the sound and have that integrated with LUIS.

Implementing smart bots

In this recipe, we are going to use Microsoft Bot Framework to create smart bots. Smart bots implement a conversation between the user and the bot. These conversations trigger a series of actions. Bots keep track of the conversation state so that it knows where it is in the conversation. Bots also keep track of the user state, or to be more precise, they keep track of the variables the user has inputted.

Bots have been used to input complex forms such as legal forms or financial documents. For our self-ordering kiosk scenario, we will be implementing a simple bot that allows someone to add food to their order. We will build upon the LUIS model we implemented in the previous recipe.

Getting ready

To test bots locally, you will need to download and install the Bot Framework Emulator from Microsoft. Installation instructions and links to documentation can be found on the GitHub page at `https://github.com/microsoft/BotFramework-Emulator`.

Next, you will need to install the dependencies. For this project, we are using Python and we have a requirements file. To install the requirements, clone the GitHub repo for this book and navigate to the `Ch7/SmartBot` folder. Then, enter the following `pip install` script:

```
pip3 install -r requirements.txt
```

This will install the Bot Framework components in addition to Flask, the web server platform that our bot will use, and `async.io`, an asynchronous library.

How to do it...

The steps for this recipe are as follows:

1. Create an `app.py` file and import the libraries:

   ```
   from flask import Flask,request,Response
   from botbuilder.schema import Activity
   from botbuilder.core import (
       BotFrameworkAdapter,
       BotFrameworkAdapterSettings,
       ConversationState,
       UserState,
       MemoryStorage
   )
   import asyncio
   from luisbot import LuisBot
   ```

2. Initialize the Flask web server:

   ```
   app = Flask(__name__)
   ```

3. Initialize the event loop:

```
loop = asyncio.get_event_loop()
```

4. Initialize the bot memory and conversation state as well as the user state:

```
botadaptersettings = BotFrameworkAdapterSettings("","")
botadapter = BotFrameworkAdapter(botadaptersettings)
memstore = MemoryStorage()
constate = ConversationState(memstore)
userstate = UserState(memstore)
botdialog = LuisBot(constate,userstate)
```

5. Set the URL routing:

```
@app.route("/api/messages",methods=["POST"])
```

6. Loop through the LUIS and Bot Framework logic:

```
def messages():
    if "application/json" in request.headers["content-type"]:
        body = request.json
    else:
        return Response(status = 415)

    activity = Activity().deserialize(request.json)

    auth_header = (request.headers["Authorization"] if \
                "Authorization" in request.headers else "")

    async def call_fun(turncontext):
        await botdialog.on_turn(turncontext)

    task = \
    loop.create_task(botadapter.process_activity(activity,
                                          "",call_fun))

    loop.run_until_complete(task)
```

7. Create a `luisbot.py` file and in the `luisbot.py` file, import the libraries:

```
from botbuilder.ai.luis import LuisApplication, \
LuisPredictionOptions, LuisRecognizer
from botbuilder.core import(
ConversationState
, UserState
, TurnContext
, ActivityHandler
, RecognizerResult
```

```
    , MessageFactory
    )
    from enum import Enum
```

8. Create an `Order` data store. This will serve as a place to hold our information:

```python
class EnumOrder(Enum):

    ENTREE=1
    SIDE=2
    DRINK=3
    DONE=4


class Order:
    def __init__(self):
        self.entree = ""
        self.drink=""
        self.side=""

    @property
    def Entree(self):
        return self.entree
    @Entree.setter
    def Entree(self,entree:str):
        self.entree = entree

    @property
    def Drink(self):
        return self.drink
    @Drink.setter
    def Drink(self,drink:str):
        self.drink = drink

    @property
    def Side(self):
        return self.side
    @Side.setter
    def Side(self,side:str):
        self.side = side
```

9. Add a conversation state data class. This will hold the conversation state:

```python
class ConState:
    def __init__(self):
        self.orderstatus = EnumOrder.ENTREE
    @property
    def CurrentPos(self):
```

```
        return self.orderstatus
    @CurrentPos.setter
    def EnumOrder(self,current:EnumOrder):
        self.orderstatus = current
```

10. Create a `LuisBot` class and initialize the variables:

```
class LuisBot(ActivityHandler):
    def __init__(self, constate:ConversationState,
    userstate:UserState):
        luis_app = LuisApplication("APP ID","primary starter key",\
                    "https://westus.api.cognitive.microsoft.com/")

        luis_option = LuisPredictionOptions(
            include_all_intents=True,include_instance_data=True)
        self.LuisReg = LuisRecognizer(luis_app,luis_option,True)
        self.constate = constate
        self.userstate = userstate
        self.conprop = self.constate.create_property("constate")
        self.userprop = self.userstate.create_property("userstate")
```

11. On each turn, record the current state:

```
async def on_turn(self,turn_context:TurnContext):
    await super().on_turn(turn_context)
    await self.constate.save_changes(turn_context)
    await self.userstate.save_changes(turn_context)
```

12. Set `on_message_activity` to get the state and entities from LUIS:

```
async def on_message_activity(self,turn_context:TurnContext):
    conmode = await self.conprop.get(turn_context,ConState)
    ordermode = await self.userprop.get(turn_context,Order)
    luis_result = await self.LuisReg.recognize(turn_context)
    intent = LuisRecognizer.top_intent(luis_result)
    await turn_context.send_activity(f"Top Intent : {intent}")
    retult = luis_result.properties["luisResult"]
    item = ''
    if len(retult.entities) != 0:
        await turn_context.send_activity(f" Luis Result
                                        {retult.entities[0]}")
        item = retult.entities[0].entity
```

13. Define the step logic. This will be the set of steps we need to take to complete an order:

```
if(conmode.orderstatus == EnumOrder.ENTREE):
    await turn_context.send_activity("Please enter a main \
                                     Entree")
    conmode.orderstatus = EnumOrder.SIDE
elif(conmode.orderstatus == EnumOrder.SIDE):
    ordermode.entree = item
    await turn_context.send_activity("Please enter a side \
                                     dish")
    conmode.orderstatus = EnumOrder.DRINK
elif(conmode.orderstatus == EnumOrder.DRINK):
    await turn_context.send_activity("Please a drink")
    ordermode.side = item
    conmode.orderstatus = EnumOrder.DONE
elif(conmode.orderstatus == EnumOrder.DONE):
    ordermode.drink = item
    info = ordermode.entree + " " + ordermode.side + \
           " " + ordermode.drink
    await turn_context.send_activity(info)
    conmode.orderstatus = EnumOrder.ENTREE
```

How it works...

Bot Framework is a bot building framework developed by Microsoft. It consists of activities and states. There are many different types of activities, such as messaging, events, and end of the conversation. For keeping track of the state, there are two variables, which are UserState and ConversationState. The user state captures information the user inputted. In our example, this is the food order. The conversation state allows the bot to ask questions in sequential order.

There's more...

Bot Framework keeps track of the conversation state and user data but that is not limited to one conversation. You can, for example, use LUIS to determine that the intent may be of a different conversation. In our ordering scenario, you can allow users to start ordering and then allow them to ask for nutritional information or the current cost of their order. In addition, you can add text-to-speech to add a voice output for the kiosk.

Creating a custom voice

The state of voice technology has come a long way in recent years. A few years ago, synthetic voices were easy to recognize. They all had the same voice font, had a robotic sound, and were monotone, so they had trouble expressing emotion. Today, we can create custom voice fonts and add emphasis, speed, and sentiment to them. In this recipe, we will go over creating a custom voice font from your voice or some actor's voice.

Getting ready

To create a custom voice font, we are going to use Microsoft's Custom Voice service. To get started, go to `https://speech.microsoft.com/portal` and click on **Custom Voice**. When on the **Custom Voice** page, click on **New project**:

Then, after giving your project a name and description, it is time to upload some audio files for training. As of the time of writing this book, the best voice system, **Neural Voice**, is in private preview. This means you will have to request access to use it. If you can access the Neural Voice feature, you will need 1 hour of voice data. To achieve a slightly less high-fidelity voice font, you can use the standard voice training system. You can provide it with as low as 1 hour of audio samples but to achieve high quality, you will need 8 hours of audio.

After creating a new project, you will be in Microsoft Speech Studio. First, click on **Data**, and then **Upload data**. Then, select **audio only**, unless you have some pre-transcribed audio:

Then, upload all of your .mp3 files zipped into one file. Depending on the amount of audio you have, it may take several hours to process the audio. Then, select the **Training** tab and click on **Train Model**. You will have the option of three different training methods: **Statistical parametric**, **Concatenative**, and **Neural**:

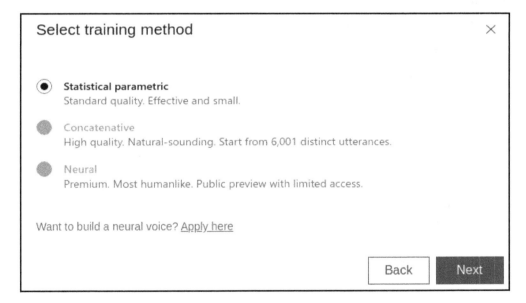

Choose the method that is the best one available to you. **Statistical parametric** is the lowest-quality option. It also requires the least amount of data. The next method, **Concatenative**, requires several hours of audio. Finally, the highest-quality option is **Neural**, for which training can take several hours.

After training is complete, head over to the **Testing** tab and test your new voice. In the **Testing** tab, you can hear and download audio. You can use text to produce audio or **Speech Synthesis Markup Language (SSML)**, which is an XML-based voice markup language. SSML allows you, if you are working with neural voices, to add sentiment such as cheerful and empathetic. In addition, it allows you to fine-tune pronunciation, emphasis, and speed.

After you have tested your custom voice, go over to the **Deployment** tab and deploy your voice. This can also take a while to process. Once it is done, go to the deployment information. You will need this information to send the request to Cognitive Services.

How to do it...

The steps for this recipe are as follows:

1. Import the libraries:

```
import requests
from playsound import playsound
```

2. Set the variables. These are the keys and variables that we retrieved in the *Getting ready* section:

```
Endpoint_key = "you will find this in your deployment"
location = 'the location you deployed it like australiaeast'
deploymentid = 'you will find this in your deployment'
project_name = 'The name you gave to your entire project'
text = "Hey, this is a custom voice demo for Microsoft's Custom
Voice"
```

3. Generate a token:

```
def get_token():
    fetch_token_url = f"https://{location}.api.cognitive.microsoft\
    .com/sts/v1.0/issueToken"
    headers = {
            'Ocp-Apim-Subscription-Key': Endpoint_key
        }
    response = requests.post(fetch_token_url, headers=headers)
    access_token = str(response.text)
    return access_token
```

4. Send a request to the custom voice with the words we want it to create and return the response:

```
constructed_url = f"https://{location}.voice.speech.microsoft\
.com/cognitiveservices/v1?deploymentId={deploymentid}"
headers = {
    'Authorization': 'Bearer ' + get_token(),
    'Content-Type': 'application/ssml+xml',
    'X-Microsoft-OutputFormat': 'riff-24khz-16bit-mono-pcm',
    'User-Agent': project_name
}

body = f"""<speak version=\"1.0\"
xmlns=\"http://www.w3.org/2001/10/synthesis\"
xmlns:mstts=\"http://www.w3.org/2001/mstts\" xml:lang=\"en-US\">
<voice name=\"Siraj\">{text}</voice></speak>"""

response = requests.post(constructed_url, headers=headers,
                         data=body)
```

5. From the response, we save the `.wav` file and then play it:

```
if response.status_code == 200:
    with open('sample.wav', 'wb') as audio:
        audio.write(response.content)
        playsound('sample.wav')
        print("\nStatus code: " + str(response.status_code) +
            "\nYour TTS is ready for playback.\n")
else:
    print("\nStatus code: " + str(response.status_code) +
        "\nSomething went wrong. Check your subscription\
    key and headers.\n")
```

How it works...

In this recipe, we used Cognitive Service's custom speech-to-text feature. Custom speech-to-text both has pretrained voice fonts and allows you to create your own custom voice fonts. Behind the scenes, it takes the voice input, then uses speech-to-text to parse words from the text, and then uses the set of words and voice to create a custom voice. After the training is complete, you can expose an endpoint to retrieve the audio from the speech model.

Enhancing bots with QnA Maker

Microsoft's QnA Maker is a tool that can take **frequently asked questions** (**FAQs**) and turn them into a set of questions and answers using language understanding, allowing users to ask questions differently to get an answer that matches up to the question. **QnA Maker** can take in a list of **tab-separated values** (**TSVs**), an FAQ web page, and a PDF, to name a few. In this recipe, we will use a TSV with questions and answers.

QnA Maker solves the fuzzy logic of interpreting speech and determining the user's question. As part of the Cognitive Service speech ecosystem, it can be incorporated easily with Bot Framework and voice to give customers a rich interactive experience.

Getting ready

Before using QnA Maker, you need a series of questions and answers. You can either point it at a website and have it parse the questions and answers or upload a TSV. For this recipe, we will use a TSV. There is a sample in the Git repo for this book.

To create a QnA Maker project, go to the QnA Maker portal at `https://www.qnamaker.ai/` and click on **Create a Knowledge Base**. It will take you through a five-step wizard to create a QnA bot. The first step deploys the resources in Azure. The second step has you choose a language and associate the bot with the new service you just created. You will then give your project a name and upload the files with questions and answers.

The most straightforward way of adding questions and answers is to use a TSV. There are a few fields you will need. These are `question`, `answer`, `source`, and `meta`. `meta` and `source` are fields you can use to query data. For example, in our nutrition FAQ, we may have several different ways of understanding and responding to a query about the calories in a burger.

After we upload and create the service, we can review what the system uploaded and add both questions and answers to existing data:

Next, we are going to click on the viewing options and select **Show meta data.** We are going to add audio we created with Speech Studio's content creator. We introduced Speech Studio in the *Creating a custom voice* recipe. In the meta tag section, we are going to add the audio files we created with the content creator:

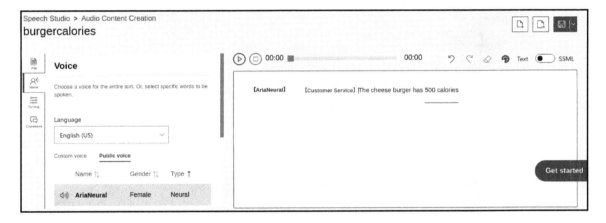

The next step is to select the **Save and Train** button and after your model has been saved, select the **Test** button and chat with your QnA Maker bot. Once you are satisfied with your QnA Maker bot, select the **Publish** button. After the training completes, QnA Maker will display curl commands to send a question to QnA Maker. From here, we will extract the keys needed to turn the request into a Python string.

How to do it...

The steps for this recipe are as follows:

1. Import the libraries needed to send web requests and play sounds:

```
import requests
import json
from playsound import playsound
```

2. Set the variables. The key and project URL can be found in the *Getting ready* section:

```
auth = 'EndpointKey '
question = 'how many calories in a cheese burger'
projectURL = ''
```

3. Generate the data in the correct format:

```
headers = {
    'Authorization': auth,
    'Content-type': 'application/json',
}

data = '{ "question":"'+question+'"}'
```

4. Send a request to the speech services at the project URL:

```
response = requests.post(projectURL, headers=headers, data=data)
json_data = json.loads(response.text)
```

5. Extract the audio from the response and play it on the speakers:

```
for meta in json_data['answers'][0]['metadata']:
    if meta['name'] == "file":
        audiofile = 'audio/' + meta['value']
        print(audiofile)
        playsound(audiofile)
```

How it works...

Under the hood, QnA Maker uses machine learning to train a model based on the question-answer pairs. It then parses the incoming text to determine which of the questions the customer was asking. In our kiosk example, QnA Maker is used to answer simple questions such as the nutritional value of the food and the location of the restaurant's information.

In this recipe, we are using the QnA Maker service to access the trained model. QnA Maker is accessed via `http post`. The results from QnA Maker are converted to sound files and played on the speakers.

There's more...

Chit-chat is incorporated in QnA Maker. To enable it, when you create a QnA Maker project, there is an option for chit-chat. Chit-chat allows users to enter a larger set of questions and have the bot make casual conversation. There are several personalities for chit-chat, such as professional and conversational.

8
Optimizing with Microcontrollers and Pipelines

Most IoT devices run on **microcontroller units** (**MCUs**), while most machine learning happens on CPUs. One of the most cutting-edge innovations in AI is the ability to run models on constrained devices. In the past, AI was limited to large computers with traditional operating systems such as Windows or Linux. Now, small devices can execute machine learning models with technologies such as ONYX and TensorFlow Lite. These constrained devices are low cost, can use machine learning without an internet connection, and can save dramatically on cloud costs.

Many IoT projects fail due to high cloud costs. IoT devices are often sold for a fixed price without a reoccurring subscription model. They then incur high cloud costs by performing machine learning or analytics. There is no reason this needs to be the case. Even for microcontrollers, the cost can be dramatically reduced by pushing machine learning and analytics to the device itself.

In this chapter, we are going to focus on two different development boards. The first is the **ESP32**, while the second is the **STM32**. The ESP32 is an MCU with Wi-Fi capabilities. They typically cost between $5 - $10 and are great for smaller projects where a few sensors need to be added to a device. An example of this would be a weather station. In contrast, the **STM32** development boards are typically used by electrical engineers to quickly start a project. There are dozens of different types of development boards but they use different compute modules such as the Cortext M0, M4, and M7. In terms of the ESP32, electrical engineers typically use them as the compute on their IoT devices. Other platforms, such as the STM32, are considered starter kits. Electrical engineers use them to determine the chipset needed and then design their own boards that specifically meet their needs.

Getting these boards running, talking to the cloud, and run ML models are non-trivial. This chapter focuses on getting the devices to perform complex computations and connecting to the cloud. To do this, we will explore the specific tools that are needed. Machine learning is typically done in higher-level languages such as Python, while the devices usually use C or C++.

The following recipes will be covered in this chapter:

- Introduction to ESP32 with IoT
- Implementing an ESP32 environment monitor
- Optimizing hyperparameters
- Dealing with BOM changes
- Building machine learning pipelines with sklearn
- Streaming machine learning with Spark and Kafka
- Enriching data using Kafka's KStreams and KTables

Let's get started!

Introduction to ESP32 with IoT

In this recipe, we'll use an ESP32 to interface with Azure IoT Hub. Using a low-level device, we will code up the network interface. We will also need to deploy code to the ESP32 from a computer and then use a serial monitor to view the results.

Getting ready

In this recipe, we are going to use the Arduino framework to program a bare-metal IoT solution. On your PC, you will need to install the Arduino **integrated development environment (IDE)**. This will install the supporting software so that we can program the ESP32 using the Arduino framework. Next, we will install **Visual Studio Code (VS Code)**. The VS Code IDE has an extension that makes board selection and library add-in easy. It also has a serial monitor and several built-in tools.

Once you have installed the Arduino IDE and VS Code, you need to find the required extension tool in VS Code. Then search for `platformIO`, as shown in the following screenshot:

Once you've installed **PlatformIO IDE**, connect your ESP32 to your computer via USB. Then, find the **PlatformIO** button in the left panel. Next, from the **Quick Access** menu, click on **Open**:

From here, you can find the main PlatformIO window and click on **Open Project**:

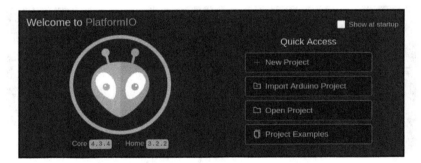

The startup wizard will take you through choosing a name for your project, a framework (**Arduino**, in our case), and a board type. For the pinouts to work correctly, you must choose the right board type. Some boards have markings on them that will allow you to look up the board types, while others will not. For that reason, when purchasing an ESP32, it is important that you can determine the board's type:

Optionally, you can change where the project is stored.

Next, you will need to install the Azure IoT Hub libraries and quickstart code. Go back to the **Quick Access** menu and click **Libraries.** Then, type Azure IoT into the search menu and click on the **AzureIoTHub** library from Microsoft. Once you've done this, change the release version to the latest that's available and click **Install.** Then, you need to do the same for the **AzureIoTUtility, WiFi,** and **AzureIoTProtocol_MQTT** libraries.

Then, go back to the **AzureIoTHub** library. There is some quickstart code here that will allow you to quickly connect to the local Wi-Fi and IoT Hub. For this recipe, we will use some sample code to test our connection to IoT Hub. In the **Examples** section, you will find three code files called iothub_II_telemetry_sample, sample_init, and iot_configs, as shown in the following screenshot. Take the code from iothub_II_telemetry_sample and replace the main.cpp code in the source code. Next, create two new files called sample_init.h and iot_configs.h and paste the example code from the PlatformIO example:

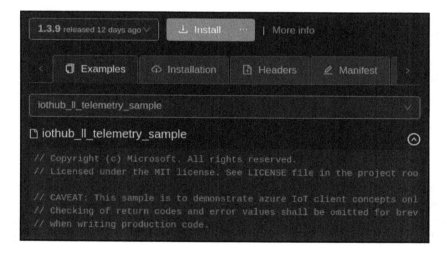

How to do it...

The steps for this recipe are as follows:

1. Add your Wi-Fi connection string. Change the strings on lines 10 and 11 of the iot_configs.h file:

```
#define IOT_CONFIG_WIFI_SSID "IoT_Net"
#define IOT_CONFIG_WIFI_PASSWORD "password1234"
```

2. Get a device connection string from Azure IoT Hub and insert it on line 19 of `iot_configs.h`:

```
#define DEVICE_CONNECTION_STRING "HostName=myhub.azure-
devices.net;DeviceId=somerandomname;SharedAccessKey=TWnLEcXf/sxZoac
Zry0akx7knPOa2gSojrkZ7oyafx0="
```

3. With your ESP32 attached to your computer via a USB, click on the **PlatformIO** icon in the left panel and then click on **Upload and Monitor**:

How it works...

Here, we uploaded the code to the ESP32 and enabled the serial monitor. The lower panel in Visual Studio should start displaying text when it has connected to a Wi-Fi network and sent messages to IoT Hub. We also created some sample code for receiving cloud-to-device messages.

There's more...

In this recipe, we have only scratched the surface of what the IoT Hub SDK is capable of doing. For example, we could even send cloud-to-device messages that allow us to queue up a set of messages for the device to digest. We could have also sent a direct message. This is like a cloud-to-device message that sends a message to a device but does not queue the message. If a device is offline, the message never gets sent. Another option would have been to upload to a blob. This allows us to upload log or binary files securely and directly to blob storage. Finally, we could have used device twins, which allow us to have a configuration file set on the device and can be queried across a fleet of devices. This would help us find out if an update did not work or a setting did not get set properly.

Implementing an ESP32 environment monitor

Setting up a simple environment monitor using hardware is fairly straightforward. In this recipe, we are going to take a proof of concept with some simple hardware attached to it. In the *There's more...* section, we will talk about how to take a design like this and go to production with it, even if you don't have **electrical engineers** (**EEs**) on your team. To do this, we are going to introduce **Fritzing**, a hardware designer. Although it is not as powerful as **KiCad** or **Altuim Designer**, it is a tool that a person who is not an electrical engineer can give to an EE or a manufacturing partner and get circuit boards designed and printed.

The goal of this recipe is not really to show you how to create a temperature and humidity sensor. Temperature and humidity sensors are the *Hello World* of IoT. Instead, this recipe focuses on implementing these on constrained devices in a rapid way via manufacturing. Not all IoT projects can be done this way. There are certainly IoT projects that require EEs to build out complex devices, such as one with a video display and sound, or high-speed devices such as those used in the medical industry.

Getting ready

In this recipe, we are going to build off of the previous recipe. We are going to use an ESP32 and must have the Arduino IDE and VS Code installed. In VS Code, we are going to add the `PlatformIO` extension. Eventually, we are going to attach the ESP32 to the computer we are using via USB but until we attach the sensor, leave it unattached. For this recipe, you will need a DHT11 digital humidity and temperature sensor, jumper cables, a 10k ohm resistor, and a breadboard. You should be able to purchase all of these components for around $20.

From here, we will need to go into VS Code and, using the `PlatformIO` extension, create a new project. Then, you will need to install the DHT sensor library from the `PlatformIO` library manager. You will then need to download Fritzing. It is an open source program. You can contribute to the project on their website and receive a copy, but you can also go to GitHub and, under **Releases**, download and install the program. The ESP32 comes in numerous hardware versions. Your ESP32 may have different pins and capabilities. The datasheet for your ESP32 will tell you what pins it has. For example, there are pins that can do things with clock cycles or voltage measurements. There's also power and ground on various pins. These are used to power external sensors. By reviewing the DHT11 and ESP32, you can create a mapping from the inputs and outputs of various components.

How to do it...

The steps for this recipe are as follows:

1. Open Fritzing and on the right-hand side panel's **Parts** section, click on the menu and select **Import...**. Then, select the ESP32 and DHT11. Both of these can be found in the source code for this chapter:

2. Search for a resistor in the **Parts** list. Once you've dragged it onto the screen, adjust its properties to **4.7kΩ**:

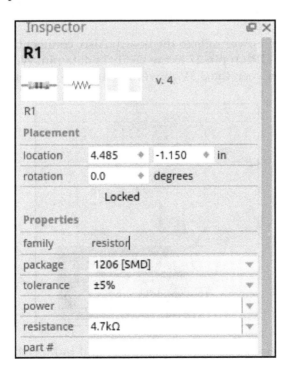

3. Now, place the DTH11 on the board and hook up the power rails using 3.3 volts and a ground:

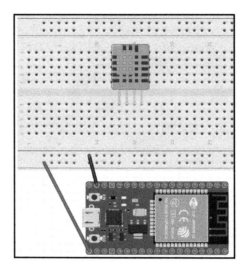

4. Then, attach the power rails to the board. Also, connect the **General-Purpose Input/Output** (**GPIO**) pin 27 to the DHT11s data pin. We must also add a 4.7k ohm resistor between the 3.3V power rail and the data pin on the DHT11:

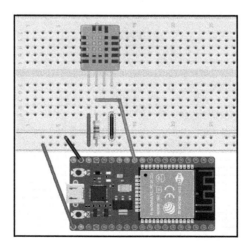

5. Next, connect the ESP32 to your computer and pull up the /src/main.cpp file from the PlatformIO project we started in the *Getting ready* section.

6. In `main.cpp`, include the `DHT.h` library reference:

```
#include "DHT.h"
```

7. Create references to your data pin on the ESP32 and the DHT sensor type:

```
#define DHTPIN 27
#define DHTTYPE DHT11
```

8. Initialize the `DHT` variable:

```
DHT dht(DHTPIN, DHTTYPE);
```

9. Set up the serial port and print a test message. Then, initialize the `dht` object:

```
void setup()
{
    Serial.begin(115200);
    Serial.println("DHT11 sensor!");
    dht.begin();
}
```

10. In the main loop, read the temperature and humidity sensors. Then, call out to the printing section and wait 2 seconds before continuing the loop:

```
void loop() {
    float h = dht.readHumidity();
    float t = dht.readTemperature();
    printResults(h,t);
    delay(2000);
}
```

11. Create a function that checks for errors. If none are found, print the results:

```
void printResults(float h,float t)
{
    if (isnan(h) || isnan(t)) {
    Serial.println("Failed to read from DHT sensor!");
    return;
}
Serial.print("Humidity: ");
Serial.print(h);
Serial.print(" %\t");
Serial.print("Temperature: ");
Serial.print(t);
Serial.println(" *C ");
}
```

How it works...

Here, the temperature and humidity sensors get power and ground from the ESP32. Once we ensured this happens, we specified a data GPIO pin and added a resistor to match up the voltages.

When you purchase a DHT11, some come with three pins, while others come with four. You can adjust these pins based on the pinout specification for the sensor. Similarly, different manufactures of the ESP32 have different pinout specifications. Before working with any hardware, it is always important to check the datasheets of that particular product.

There's more...

At this point, we have a working prototype. There are several paths you can take to get the boards designed and the product mass-produced in a factory. You can hire EEs to do this, but for something this small, you can often go to a company that specializes in board design, such as Seeed Studios. Many manufacturing plants offer a hardware designing service that can take the Fritzing sketch and turn it into a product. These manufacturing plants can often print out prototypes and mass-produce the boards when you are ready.

Optimizing hyperparameters

There are many different ways of tuning hyperparameters. If we were to do this manually, we could put random variables into our parameters and see which one was the best. To do this, we could perform a grid-wise approach, where we map the possible options and put in some random tries and keep going down a route that seems to produce the best outcomes. We might use statistics or machine learning to help us determine what parameters can give us the best results. These different approaches have pros and cons, depending on the shape of the loss of the experiment.

There are various machine learning libraries that can help us perform these types of common tasks easier. `sklearn`, for example, has a `RandomizedSearchCV` method that, given a set of parameters, will perform a search for the best model with the least loss. In this recipe, we will expand on the *Classifying chemical sensors with decision trees* recipe from `Chapter 3`, *Machine Learning for IoT*, and use a random forest. However, we will also add a grid search in order to optimize our results.

Getting ready

In this recipe, we will be using the MOX sensor dataset from `Chapter 3`, *Machine Learning for IoT*. There, we saved our data in Delta Lake. Due to this, we can pull it easily into our Spark Notebook. We will also be using the `koalas`, `sklearn`, and `numpy` Python packages.

How to do it...

The steps for this recipe are as follows:

1. Import the necessary libraries:

```
import koalas as pd
import numpy as np

from sklearn.model_selection import train_test_split
from sklearn.ensemble import RandomForestClassifier
from sklearn.model_selection import GridSearchCV
```

2. Import the data from Databricks Delta Lake:

```
df = spark.sql("select * from ChemicalSensor where class <>
'banana'")
pdf = df.toPandas()
```

3. Select and encode the data:

```
from sklearn.preprocessing import OneHotEncoder
from sklearn.preprocessing import LabelEncoder

pdf.rename(columns = {'class':'classification'}, inplace = True)
X = pdf
y = pdf['classification']

label_encoder = LabelEncoder()

integer_encoded = \
label_encoder.fit_transform(pdf['classification'])
onehot_encoder = OneHotEncoder(sparse=False)

integer_encoded = integer_encoded.reshape(len(integer_encoded), 1)
onehot_encoded = onehot_encoder.fit_transform(integer_encoded)

feature_cols = ['r1', 'r2', 'r4', 'r5', 'r6','r7', 'r8', 'temp',
                'humidity', 't0', 'td']
X = pdf[feature_cols]
```

```
y = onehot_encoded

X_train, X_test, y_train, y_test = \
train_test_split(X, y, test_size=0.3, random_state=40)
```

4. Select the parameters you wish to tune:

```
model_params = {
    'n_estimators': [50, 150, 250],
    'max_features': ['sqrt', 0.25, 0.5, 0.75, 1.0],
    'min_samples_split': [2, 4, 6]
}
```

5. Create an instance of the random forest classifier algorithm so that we can adjust its hyperparameters later:

```
rf_model = RandomForestClassifier(random_state=1)
```

6. Set up a grid search estimator so that we can tune our parameters:

```
clf = GridSearchCV(rf_model, model_params, cv=5)
```

7. Train the decision tree classifier:

```
model = clf.fit(X_train,y_train)
```

8. Predict the response for the test dataset:

```
y_pred = clf.predict(X_test)
```

9. Print the winning set of hyperparameters:

```
from pprint import pprint
pprint(model.best_estimator_.get_params())
```

How it works...

This algorithm is an easy to implement algorithm that we worked with in Chapter 3, *Machine Learning for IoT*. There, we took a random stab at choosing an algorithm. Then, we had it go through one run of the code to get the necessary output. In this recipe, however, we caused it to run through many more runs to find the best estimator we could find. We could have done the same thing using a spreadsheet to keep track of all of the runs. However, this allows us to automate the process of performing experiments and tracking the results.

Dealing with BOM changes

Bill of Materials (**BOMs**) are the components that make up the device. These can be resistors, chips, and other components. The life cycle of a typical IoT product is about 10 years. In that time, things can change with the product. A component manufacturer could discontinue a part such as a chip line. Outsourced manufacturers typically perform BOM optimization on a board layout, though BOM optimization can change the quality of the device. For example, it can change the sensitivity of the sensor or the lifetime of a device.

This can throw off trained models and can have a dramatic effect on any remaining useful life calculations and predictive maintenance models. When working with IoT and machine learning, tracking changes that have been made to any remaining useful life based on BOM and factory changes can help us detect issues with the quality and longevity of a device.

This is typically done with a database. When a device is made in a factory, that device's serial number, BOM version, and factory details are stored in that factory. This is where a total expected lifespan can be applied to the device.

Getting ready

In this recipe, we are going to spin up a Docker instance of a SQL Server database. To get started, you must install Docker.

The next step is to build and run a SQL Server database using `docker`:

```
docker pull mcr.microsoft.com/mssql/server:2017-latest
```

Then, run the Docker container:

```
docker run -e 'ACCEPT_EULA=Y' -e 'MSSQL_AGENT_ENABLED=true' \
-e 'MSSQL_PID=Standard' -e 'SA_PASSWORD=Password!' \
-p 1433:1433 --name sqlserver_1 \
-d mcr.microsoft.com/mssql/server:2017-latest
```

Now that we have a working SQL Server database, we need to add a database and two tables for it. You can connect to the SQL database by installing the `mssql` plugin for VS Code and then connecting to the database with the username and password we had in the Docker file:

Once you've done this, click on the new SQL Server tool in the left panel. Then, click on the plus (**+**) button to be taken through a wizard that will help you create a database connection. When the wizard asks you for the **ado.net** connection string type in `localhost`, it will ask you for a username and password. Type in `sa` for the username and `Password!` for the password.

Then, run the following SQL statements by clicking on the green arrow in the upper right of the screen:

```
CREATE DATABASE MLTracking
GO
USE MLTracking
GO
CREATE TABLE Product(
  productid INTEGER IDENTITY(1,1) NOT NULL PRIMARY KEY,
  productName VARCHAR(255) NOT NULL,
  BeginLife Datetime NOT NULL,
EndLife Datetime NULL,
  );
GO
CREATE TABLE RUL(
```

```
    RULid INTEGER IDENTITY(1,1) NOT NULL PRIMARY KEY,
ProductId int,
TotalRULDays int,
DateCalculated datetime not null
)
GO
```

From here, `pip` install `pyodbc` from `pypi` and create a new Python script in VS Code.

How to do it...

The steps for this recipe are as follows:

1. Import the `pyodbc` library:

   ```
   import pyodbc
   ```

2. Connect to the database:

   ```
   conn = pyodbc.connect('Driver={SQL Server};'
    'Server=localhost;'
    'Database=MLTracking;'
    'uid=sa;'
    'pwd=Password!;')
   ```

3. Create a database connection cursor so that you can run queries:

   ```
   cursor = conn.cursor()
   ```

4. Insert the product and manufacturing date into the `Device` table and commit the transaction:

   ```
   cursor.execute('''
     INSERT INTO MLTracking.dbo.Product (Product,BeginLife)
     VALUES
     ('Smoke Detector 9000',GETDATE()),
     ''')
   conn.commit()
   ```

5. Once you've calculated the remaining useful life of that product, add that information to the database:

   ```
   cursor.execute('''
     INSERT INTO MLTracking.dbo.RUL
   (ProductId,TotalRULDays,DateCalculated )
     VALUES
   ```

```
        (1,478,GETDATE()),
        ''')
conn.commit()
```

How it works...

In this recipe, we showed you how to use a database to track your results over time. Databases allow us to insert and update information about our models over time.

There's more...

In this example, we looked at products. Tracking the end life of devices can give our models real-world feedback and lets us know when they should be retrained. We can store the predicted error or loss rate and compare it against real-world devices.

Building machine learning pipelines with sklearn

The `sklearn pipeline` package makes it easy for us to manage multiple stages of feature engineering and modeling. Performing machine learning experiments is more just than training models. It is a combination of several factors. First, you need to cleanse and transform the data. Then, you must enrich the data with feature engineering. These common tasks can be built up into a series of steps called a **pipeline**. When we're trying out different variants on our experiments, we can use these pipelines to train a series of very complex steps so that they become something simple and manageable that can be reused.

Getting ready

In this recipe, we are going to use the data that was previously feature engineered in the *Enhancing data using feature engineering* recipe of `Chapter 4`, *Deep Learning for Predictive Maintenance*. In that recipe, we put data into Databricks and then cleansed that data so that we could use it in additional experiments. To retrieve this data, we are simply going to use a `select` statement from Delta Lake. For this recipe, you will need `pandas` and `sklearn` installed on your Spark cluster.

How to do it...

The steps for this recipe are as follows:

1. Import `pandas` and `sklearn`:

```
import pandas as pd
from sklearn.pipeline import Pipeline
from sklearn.impute import SimpleImputer
from sklearn.preprocessing import StandardScaler, OneHotEncoder
from sklearn.ensemble import RandomForestClassifier
from sklearn.compose import ColumnTransformer
```

2. Import the data from Delta Lake:

```
train = spark.sql("select * from engine").toPandas()
train.drop(columns="label" , inplace=True)
test = spark.sql("select * from engine_test2").toPandas()
```

3. Create transformers that convert data into standardized numeric or categorical data:

```
numeric_transformer = Pipeline(steps=[
    ('imputer', SimpleImputer(strategy='median')),
    ('scaler', StandardScaler())])
categorical_transformer = Pipeline(steps=[
    ('imputer', SimpleImputer(strategy='constant',
                              fill_value='missing')),
    ('onehot', OneHotEncoder(handle_unknown='ignore'))])
```

4. Extract the necessary features and create a processor:

```
numeric_features = \
train.select_dtypes(include=['int64', 'float64']).columns
categorical_features = \
train.select_dtypes(include=['object']).drop(['cycle'],
                                    axis=1).columns

preprocessor = ColumnTransformer(
    transformers=[
        ('num', numeric_transformer, numeric_features),
        ('cat', categorical_transformer, categorical_features)])
```

5. Create a random forest pipeline step:

```
rf = Pipeline(steps=[('preprocessor', preprocessor),
                     ('classifier', RandomForestClassifier())])
```

6. Fit the classifier:

```
rf.fit(X_train, y_train)
```

7. Perform the classification:

```
y_pred = rf.predict(X_test)
```

How it works...

Building machine learning pipelines is very common in data science. It helps simplify complex operations and adds a level of reusability to the software code. In this recipe, we used `sklearn` to perform complex operations on a simple pipeline. In our pipeline, we created a set of transformers. For the numeric numbers, we used a scaler, while for the categorical numbers, we used one-hot encoding. Next, we created a processor pipeline. In our case, we used a random forest classifier. Note that this pipeline step is an array, so we could pass more classifiers into our array. However, for the sake of simplicity, we will save that for the *There's more...* section. Finally, we trained and got the predictions from our model.

There's more...

As we mentioned in the introduction to this recipe, the purpose of pipelines is to enable you to tweak your pipeline steps easily. In this section, we are going to tweak those steps to help us achieve a higher accuracy rate. In this case, we are simply going to extend the preceding code and add a classifier array of machine learning algorithms. From there, we will score the model so that we can determine which one was the best. The code for this is as follows:

```
from sklearn.metrics import accuracy_score, log_loss
from sklearn.neighbors import KNeighborsClassifier
from sklearn.tree import DecisionTreeClassifier
from sklearn.ensemble import RandomForestClassifier, AdaBoostClassifier,
GradientBoostingClassifier
from sklearn.discriminant_analysis import LinearDiscriminantAnalysis
from sklearn.discriminant_analysis import QuadraticDiscriminantAnalysis
classifiers = [
    KNeighborsClassifier(3),
    DecisionTreeClassifier(),
    RandomForestClassifier(),
    AdaBoostClassifier(),
    GradientBoostingClassifier()
    ]
```

```
for classifier in classifiers:
    pipe = Pipeline(steps=[('preprocessor', preprocessor),
                           ('classifier', classifier)])
    pipe.fit(X_train, y_train)
    print(classifier)
    print("model score: %.3f" % pipe.score(X_test, y_test))
```

Streaming machine learning with Spark and Kafka

Kafka is a real-time streaming message hub. Combined with Kafka, Databrick's ability to ingest streams and perform machine learning on them in real time allows you to perform powerful machine learning in near real time. In this recipe, we are going to use Confluent. Confluent is the company that was founded by the creators of Kafka. They have a cloud offering on Azure, GCP, and AWS. We are also going to use Databricks, which is available on Azure, GCP, and AWS.

Getting ready

In the cloud marketplace, spin up Confluent and Databricks. This will give you a Kafka and Spark system that is elastically scalable. Once you've spinned up these systems, go to the Confluent website at `https://confluent.cloud` and enter the username and password you set up in the cloud marketplace. Then, click on **Create cluster**. Follow the wizard to create your first cluster. Once you are in your cluster, click on **API access** in the menu. Then, find the **Create key** button that will allow you to create an API access key:

Once you've created a key, jot down its username and password; you will need these details later.

Next, go to the **Topics** section and, using the **Create topic** button, create two topics: one called `Turbofan` and another called `Turbofan_RUL`. Next, we will create a Python file so that we can test our new topic. Create a Python file with the following code to produce a message for the `TurboFan` topic:

```python
from confluent_kafka import Producer
from datetime import datetime as dt
import json
import time

producer = Producer({
    'bootstrap.servers': "pkc-lgwgm.eastus2.azure.confluent.cloud:9092",
    'security.protocol': 'SASL_SSL',
    'sasl.mechanism': "PLAIN",
    "sasl.username": "",
    "sasl.password": "",
    'auto.offset.reset': 'earliest'
})

data = json.dumps({'Record_ID':1,'Temperature':'100','Vibration':120,
                   'age':1000, 'time':time.time()})
producer.send('TurboFan', data)
```

Now, you can go to your topic in the Confluent Cloud UI and watch for messages on that topic by selecting the topic (**TurboFan**) and then **Messages**:

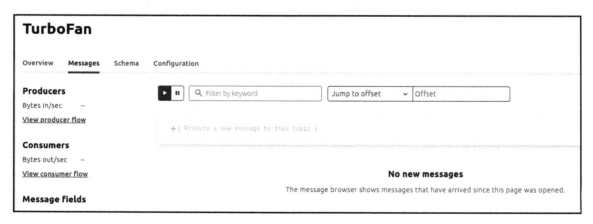

If you run the preceding code, you will see a message going to Kafka.

How to do it...

The steps for this recipe are as follows:

1. Stream Kafka into Databricks. In a Databricks notebook, enter the following code:

    ```
    from pyspark.sql.types import StringType
    import json
    import pandas as pd
    from sklearn.linear_model import LogisticRegression

     df.readStream.format("kafka")
    .option("kafka.bootstrap.servers", "...azure.confluent.cloud:9092")
    .option("subscribe", "TurboFan")
    .option("startingOffsets", "latest")
    .option("kafka.security.protocol","SASL_SSL")
    .option("kafka.sasl.mechanism", "PLAIN")
    .option("kafka.sasl.jaas.config",
    "kafkashaded.org.apache.kafka.common.security.plain.PlainLoginModul
    e required username=\"Kafka UserName\" password=\"Kafka
    Password\";")
    .load()
    .select($"value")
    .withColumn("Value", $"value".cast(StringType))
    ```

2. Specify the fields from the JSON file to serialize them as objects:

    ```
    val jsDF1 = kafka1.select( get_json_object($"Value",
    "$.Temperature").alias("Temp"),
    get_json_object($"Value", "$.Vibration").alias("Vibration")
    ,get_json_object($"Value", "$.age").alias("Age")
    )
    ```

3. Define the function that will do the inference:

    ```
    def score(row):
        d = json.loads(row)
        p = pd.DataFrame.from_dict(d, orient = "index").transpose()
        pred = model.predict_proba(p.iloc[:,0:10])[0][0]
        result = {'Record_ID': d['Record_ID'], 'pred': pred }
        return str(json.dumps(result))
    ```

4. Perform inference using the UDF and save the results in a DataFrame:

    ```
    df = df.selectExpr("CAST(value AS STRING)")
    score_udf = udf(score, StringType())
    df = df.select( score_udf("value").alias("value"))
    ```

5. Write the devices that are failing to a different DataFrame:

```
failure_df = df.filter(df.value > 0.9)
```

6. Stream that DataFrame back to Kafka as a new topic and write the results to Kafka:

```
query = df.writeStream.format("kafka")
.option("kafka.bootstrap.servers", "{external_ip}:9092")
.option("topic", "Turbofan_Failure")
.option("kafka.security.protocol","SASL_SSL")
.option("kafka.sasl.mechanism", "PLAIN")
.option("kafka.sasl.jaas.config",
"kafkashaded.org.apache.kafka.common.security.plain.PlainLoginModul
e required username=\"Kafka UserName\" password=\"Kafka
Password\";")
  .option("checkpointLocation", "/temp").start()
```

How it works...

Kafka is a streaming engine designed to handle large amounts of data. Data is ingested into Kafka and then sent to Spark, where the probability can be sent back to Kafka. In this example, we used Confluent Cloud and Databricks. These managed services can be found on all major cloud marketplaces.

In this recipe, we received real-time data from the engines. Then, we streamed that data in Spark and ran an inference on it. Once we'd received the results, we streamed them back into a separate Kafka topic. Using a Kafka topic and Kafka itself allows us to push that data into a database, data lakes, and microservices, all from a single data pipeline.

There's more...

In addition to putting all of the data into a topic so that it can be dumped into a data store, we can stream the data into an alerting system. To do this, we can make a Kafka consumer, as shown in the following code. Here, we will stream the code down to a local system and then have a `msg_process` function that we can use to write to an alert system such as **Twilio**:

```
from confluent_kafka import Consumer

conf = {'bootstrap.servers': "host1:9092,host2:9092",
        'group.id': "foo",
        'kafka.security.protocol':'SASL_SSL,
```

```
        'kafka.sasl.mechanism':'PLAIN',
        'kafka.sasl.jaas.config':
'kafkashaded.org.apache.kafka.common.security.plain.PlainLoginModule
required username=\"Kafka UserName\" password=\"Kafka Password\";')
        'auto.offset.reset': 'smallest'}

running = True
consumer = Consumer(conf)
consumer.subscribe('Turbofan_Failure')
 while running:
    msg = consumer.poll(timeout=1.0)
    if msg is None: continue
    msg_process(msg)

def msg_process(msg):
    pass
```

Enriching data using Kafka's KStreams and KTables

Often, in IoT, there are external data sources that must be included. This could be weather data that affects the performance of the device or data from other nearby devices. An easy way of doing this is to use Kafka KSQL Server. Like we did in the previous recipe, we are going to use Confluent Cloud's KSQL Server, which you can get if you have a Confluent Cloud subscription.

In this recipe, we are going to get data from a weather service topic and put it into a KTable. A KTable is similar to a database table. All data coming into Kafka comes in key-value pairs. With KTable, when data comes in with a new key, we insert it into our KTable. If it contains a key that already exists in our KTable, we update it. We are also going to convert our topic into a KStream. This allows us to run standard SQL-like queries over our table and stream. By doing this, we can, for example, query the current weather and join it to the engine data from our previous recipe. This allows us to enrich the data.

Getting ready

In the **Confluent Cloud ksqlDB** portal, go to the **ksqlDB** tab and add an application:

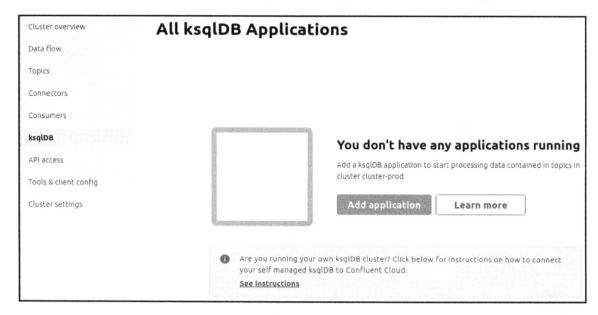

Once you've completed all the setup steps, you will have a KSQL query editor. From here, we will edit our queries.

This recipe is a continuation of the previous recipe. You will need the streaming `TurboFan` data that we set up running in Kafka. You will also need to run the `weatherstreamer.py` Kafka Weather Streamer Python script, which can be found in the `ch10` directory of the GitHub repository for this book.

Finally, you will need to go into ksqlDB, which is where you will find the query editor. We are going to use that editor to create our streams and tables.

How to do it...

The steps for this recipe are as follows:

1. Create a KTable with our weather topic:

```
CREATE TABLE users (
    TurboFanNum BIGINT PRIMARY KEY,
```

```
        temperature BIGINT,
        humidity BIGINT
    ) WITH (
        KAFKA_TOPIC = 'weather',
        VALUE_FORMAT = 'JSON'
    );
```

2. Convert the `TurboFan` topic into a data stream:

```
CREATE STREAM TurboFan (
    TurboFanNum BIGINT,
    HoursLogged BIGINT,
    VIBRATIONSCORE BIGING
) WITH (
    KAFKA_TOPIC='TurboFan',
    VALUE_FORMAT='JSON'
);
```

3. Join the table and stream to a new topic:

```
CREATE STREAM TurboFan_Enriched AS
  SELECT
    TurnboFan.TurboFanNum,
    HoursLogged,
    VIBRATIONSCORE,
    temperature,
    humidity

FROM TurboFan
  LEFT JOIN Weather ON Weather.TurboFanNum = TurboFan.TurboFanNum
EMIT CHANGES;
```

How it works...

KSQL Server is a technology built upon the Kafka Streams API. The goal of this tool is to allow data enrichment and data transformation to occur in real time. In this recipe, we took the streams and converted one into a table of the most recent keys. We used these keys to update the values in our table. Next, we took a topic and created a stream view on top of it. Finally, we joined our table to our stream and created an output as a new stream. This is also a new topic in Kafka.

There's more...

With KSQL Server, we can use more of the semantics that SQL provides, such as group by, count, and sum. Because Kafka is an unending set of data, we can use windowing to grab data by time segments. For example, we may want to know if the average temperature was over 100 degrees. We may want to look at this over a 20-second period. In KSQL, we can remote this as another stream:

```
CREATE STREAM TurboFan_ToHot AS
  SELECT
      TurnboFan.TurboFanNum,
      avg(temperature)
  FROM TurboFan_Enriched
  WINDOW TUMBLING (SIZE 20 SECONDS)
  GROUP BY TurboFanNum
  HAVING avg(temperature) > 100
  EMIT CHANGES;
```

Deploying to the Edge 9

Performing **machine learning and operations** (**MLOps**) on a single computer can be challenging. When we think about training, deploying, and maintaining models across thousands of computers, the complexity of doing so can be daunting. Luckily, there are ways of reducing this complexity using tools such as containerization and **continuous integration/continuous deployment** (**CI/CD**) pipelines. In this chapter, we are going to discuss deploying models in a way that is secure, updatable, and optimized for the hardware at hand.

In terms of building updatable models, we are going to discuss using Azure IoT Hub Edge devices to enable **over-the-air** (**OTA**) updates across a single management plane. We are also going to use device twins to maintain the fleet and push configuration settings going to our models. In addition, we'll learn how to train a model on one type of computer architecture, such as x86, and run it on ARM. Finally, we are going to discuss how to use fog computing to perform distributed machine learning across different types of devices.

This chapter consist of the following recipes:

- OTA updating MCUs
- Deploying modules with IoT Edge
- Offloading to the web with TensorFlow.js
- Deploying mobile models
- Maintaining your fleet with device twins
- Enabling distributed machine learning with fog computing

Let's get started!

OTA updating MCUs

OTA updates are essential for deploying security updates, new functionality, and updating models. There are two different techniques for OTA updates. The first is building a custom program that, ideally, runs on its own program or thread that is different than the main program you are trying to update. This software downloads the new firmware to the flash memory and registers and starts the new firmware. If the new firmware fails to start, the custom software can then start up the working version of the software. This usually involves saving half of the flash memory available for OTA updates.

The second way is to use a system such as Azure IoT Edge to update the Docker containers on the device. This requires a device that is running a full operating system, such as Raspbian, Ubuntu, or Windows. The majority of IoT devices do not have the compute needed to support IoT Edge. In this recipe, we will talk about OTA updates on MCUs, while in the next, we will discuss OTA updates with IoT Edge.

Getting ready

In this recipe, we are going to use an ESP32 to do an OTA update for a small MCU device. With the ESP32, we are going to be programming in the IDF framework. **Espressif IoT Development Framework (ESP-IDF)** is a low-level programming framework. It has fewer pre-built components than the Arduino framework but is faster and more geared to industrial applications.

For development, we are going to be using VS Code with the **PlatformIO** extension added. We can create a project by going to the **PlatformIO** home page and selecting **+ New Project**:

From there, add a project name, and then select the development board and the development framework you will be using. In my case, I am using the **NodeMCU-32S** as my development board:

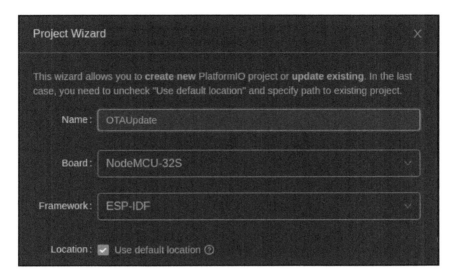

Then, rename `empty.c` to `main.c` in your root directory and start coding.

How to do it...

The steps for this recipe are as follows:

1. Import the necessary libraries:

```
#include <string.h>
#include "freertos/FreeRTOS.h"
#include "freertos/task.h"
#include "cJSON.h"
#include "driver/gpio.h"
#include "esp_system.h"
#include "esp_log.h"
#include "esp_http_client.h"
#include "esp_https_ota.h"
#include "wifi_functions.h"
```

2. Set the firmware version, certificates, and buffer size:

```
#define FIRMWARE_VERSION 0.1
#define UPDATE_JSON_URL "https://microshak.com/esp32/firmware.json"

extern const char server_cert_pem_start[]
asm("_binary_certs_pem_start");
extern const char server_cert_pem_end[]
asm("_binary_certs_pem_end");

char rcv_buffer[200];
```

3. Create an HTTP event handler:

```
esp_err_t _http_event_handler(esp_http_client_event_t *evt)
{
    switch(evt->event_id) {
        case HTTP_EVENT_ERROR:
            break;
        case HTTP_EVENT_ON_CONNECTED:
            break;
        case HTTP_EVENT_HEADER_SENT:
            break;
        case HTTP_EVENT_ON_HEADER:
            break;
        case HTTP_EVENT_ON_DATA:
            if (!esp_http_client_is_chunked_response(evt->client)){
                strncpy(rcv_buffer, (char*)evt->data, evt->data_len);
            }
            break;
        case HTTP_EVENT_ON_FINISH:
            break;
        case HTTP_EVENT_DISCONNECTED:
            break;
    }
    return ESP_OK;
}
```

4. Next, we are going to create an infinite loop (for the sake of brevity, we will forget the machine learning algorithm):

```
void ml_task(void *pvParameter)
{
    while(1)
    {
        //ML on this thread
    }
}
```

5. Check for OTA updates. Doing so will download the manifest. Then, if the version is different than the current version, it triggers a download and restarts the device:

```
void check_update_task(void *pvParameter)
{
  while(1)
  {
    printf("Looking for a new firmware...\n");
    esp_http_client_config_t config =
    {
        .url = UPDATE_JSON_URL,
        .event_handler = _http_event_handler,
    };
    esp_http_client_handle_t client =
        esp_http_client_init(&config);
    esp_err_t err = esp_http_client_perform(client);
    if(err == ESP_OK) {
      cJSON *json = cJSON_Parse(rcv_buffer);
      if(json == NULL) printf("downloaded file is not a valid json,
      aborting...\n");
      else {
        cJSON *version = cJSON_GetObjectItemCaseSensitive(json,
        "version");
        cJSON *file = cJSON_GetObjectItemCaseSensitive(json,
        "file");
        if(!cJSON_IsNumber(version)) printf("unable to read new
        version, aborting...\n");
        else {
          double new_version = version->valuedouble;
          if(new_version > FIRMWARE_VERSION) {
            printf("current firmware version (%.1f) is lower than
            the available one (%.1f), upgrading...\n",
            FIRMWARE_VERSION, new_version);
            if(cJSON_IsString(file) && (file->valuestring != NULL))
            {
              printf("downloading and installing new
                      firmware(%s)...\n", file->valuestring);
              esp_http_client_config_t ota_client_config =
              {
                .url = file->valuestring,
                .cert_pem = server_cert_pem_start,
              };
              esp_err_t ret = esp_https_ota(&ota_client_config);
              if (ret == ESP_OK)
              {
                printf("OTA OK, restarting...\n");
                esp_restart();
```

```
                        }
                        else
                        {
                          printf("OTA failed...\n");
                        }
                    }
                    else printf("unable to read the new file name,
                                aborting...\n");
                }
                else printf("current firmware version (%.1f) is greater
                            or equal to the available one (%.1f),
                            nothing to do...\n",
                            FIRMWARE_VERSION, new_version);
            }
        }
    }
    else printf("unable to download the json file, aborting...\n");
    esp_http_client_cleanup(client);
    printf("\n");
        vTaskDelay(60000 / portTICK_PERIOD_MS);
    }
}
```

6. Initialize the Wi-Fi:

```
static EventGroupHandle_t wifi_event_group;
const int CONNECTED_BIT = BIT0;

static esp_err_t event_handler(void *ctx, system_event_t *event)
{
    switch(event->event_id)
    {
      case SYSTEM_EVENT_STA_START:
            esp_wifi_connect();
            break;
      case SYSTEM_EVENT_STA_GOT_IP:
        xEventGroupSetBits(wifi_event_group, CONNECTED_BIT);
        break;
      case SYSTEM_EVENT_STA_DISCONNECTED:
        esp_wifi_connect();
        break;
      default:
        break;
    }
  return ESP_OK;
}

void wifi_initialise(void)
```

```
{
    ESP_ERROR_CHECK(nvs_flash_init());
    wifi_event_group = xEventGroupCreate();
    tcpip_adapter_init();
    ESP_ERROR_CHECK(esp_event_loop_init(event_handler, NULL));
    wifi_init_config_t wifi_init_config = WIFI_INIT_CONFIG_DEFAULT();
    ESP_ERROR_CHECK(esp_wifi_init(&wifi_init_config));
    ESP_ERROR_CHECK(esp_wifi_set_storage(WIFI_STORAGE_RAM));
    ESP_ERROR_CHECK(esp_wifi_set_mode(WIFI_MODE_STA));
    wifi_config_t wifi_config = {
        .sta = {
            .ssid = "mynetwork",
            .password = "mywifipassword",
        },
    };
    ESP_ERROR_CHECK(esp_wifi_set_config(ESP_IF_WIFI_STA,
                                        &wifi_config));
    ESP_ERROR_CHECK(esp_wifi_start());
}

void wifi_wait_connected()
{
    xEventGroupWaitBits(wifi_event_group, CONNECTED_BIT, false, true,
                        portMAX_DELAY);
}
```

7. In the main loop, initiate the Wi-Fi and create two tasks (the OTA update task and our mock machine learning task):

```
void app_main() {
    printf("HTTPS OTA, firmware %.1f\n\n", FIRMWARE_VERSION);

    wifi_initialise();
    wifi_wait_connected();
    printf("Connected to wifi network\n");

    xTaskCreate(&ml_task, "ml_task", configMINIMAL_STACK_SIZE, NULL,
                5, NULL);
    xTaskCreate(&check_update_task, "check_update_task", 8192, NULL,
                5, NULL);
}
```

How it works...

The program has three tasks. The first task is to set up and ensure that it is connected to the Wi-Fi. It will not do anything else until it establishes a connection. This program uses Free RTOS as its real-time operating system. RTOS allows threads to execute independently. This allows us to have two non-blocking threads. Our first thread performs a machine learning task, while the second performs an update task. The update task allows us to poll our web server on a less frequent basis.

There's more...

The OTA updater in this recipe needs a manifest so that it can check against its current version and find the file to download. The following is a .json file example of the manifest:

```
{
    "version":1.2.
    "file":"https://microshak.com/firmware/otaml1_2.bin"
}
```

OTA updates are an important thing for any IoT device. Most manufactures of silicon devices, such as the ESP32 or STM32, have solved this OTA update issue. These manufacturers usually have sample code that will help you quickly start your project.

Deploying modules with IoT Edge

Deploying models to the edge can be risky. In the previous recipe, we made a simple update to a small IoT device. If the update bricked the entire fleet of devices, they may be lost forever. If we had a more powerful device, then we could spin up separate programs that work independently of each other. If the update failed, the program could revert to a version that worked. That is where IoT Edge comes in. IoT Edge specifically handles the problem of running multiple programs on an IoT device by using Docker technology. This, for example, could be mining equipment that needs to perform geofencing operations, machine learning for device failure predictions, and reinforcement learning for self-driving cars. Any one of these programs could be updated without impacting the other modules.

In this recipe, we are going to use Azure's IoT Hub and IoT Edge capabilities. This will involve using Docker and IoT Hub to push models down to devices.

Getting ready

For this recipe, you will need an Azure IoT Hub and an Azure Container Registry in the cloud. You will also need **Visual Studio Code** (**VS Code**) with the Azure IoT extension installed and a Raspberry Pi. There are three main components you will need for this recipe. The first is our Raspberry Pi, which must be set up. This will involve installing Moby, a lightweight version of Docker. Next is writing the code. In our case, we will be writing the code on an x86-based laptop and deploying the models to an ARM-based Raspberry Pi. Finally, we will be deploying the code to a device or series of devices.

Setting up our Raspberry Pi

For this recipe, we are going to code on the Raspberry Pi remotely from a laptop computer. To do that, we are going to need to allow SSH and then connect to the Raspberry Pi via VS Code. On the Raspberry Pi, you will need to go to **Menu | Preferences | Raspberry Pi Configuration**. Then, click on **Interfaces** and enable **SSH**:

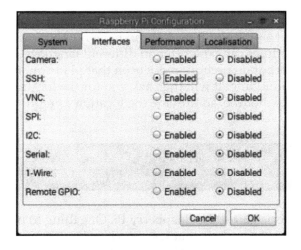

In a Terminal window, type in the following command:

```
hostname -I
```

This will give you the IP address of your Raspberry Pi. Take that IP address and, back on your desktop computer, in VS Code, install the SSH plugin and connect to the Raspberry Pi. Then, connect to the Raspberry Pi using VS Code by using the **Connect to SSH** button. From there, follow the wizard to connect to the Raspberry Pi using the device's IP address and password. Once you've done this, you can create a new project on the device.

Also, while you are on the device, you will need to install the IoT Edge agent. To do this, follow the instructions at `https://docs.microsoft.com/en-us/azure/iot-edge/how-to-install-iot-edge-linux`.

Coding setup

Now, create a new IoT Edge project. To do this, open Visual Studio and install the Azure IoT Edge extension, as well as the Docker extension. Then, using *Ctrl + Shift + P*, open the command window, type `Azure IoT Edge:` into the **Search** bar, and select **Azure IoT Edge: New IoT Edge Solution**:

Once you've done this, you will see a wizard that asks you to name the project. Then, the wizard will have you add a module. A project can have numerous modules that do different tasks. These modules can be written in different languages or use Azure Machine Learning Services to incorporate prebuilt models on that platform. In our case, we are making a custom Python module. It will then ask you for the location of the Azure Container Registry for the module, so provide the location as required, as shown in the following screenshot:

myazurecontainerregistry.azurecr.io/mynewmodule

Provide Docker Image Repository for the Module (Press 'Enter' to confirm or 'Escape' to cancel)

From here, we can develop against the Raspberry Pi. One thing to note on developing machine learning on a Raspberry Pi is that tasks such as environmental builds can take 10 times longer. A machine learning Docker build that takes minutes on a 16-core desktop with 32 GB RAM can take 10 times the duration when it is forced to compile on 1 core with 2 GB RAM.

At this point, VS Code's code generator has created a `main.py` file that has a starter template that receives a message from IoT Hub and echoes it back. In the *How to do it...* section, we will modify that to include a stub out for your machine learning code. In the *There's more...* section, we are going to talk about building the module for the ARM32 environment.

How to do it...

The steps for this recipe are as follows:

1. In the `main.py` file, import the necessary libraries:

```
import time
import os
import sys
import asyncio
from six.moves import input
import threading
from azure.iot.device.aio import IoTHubModuleClient
from azure.iot.device import Message
import uuid
```

2. Create a stub for your ML code:

```
def MLCode():
    # You bispoke ML code here
    return True
```

3. Create a message-sending function:

```
async def send_d2c_message(module_client):
    while True:
        msg = Message("test machine learning ")
        msg.message_id = uuid.uuid4()
        msg.custom_properties["MachineLearningBasedAlert"]=\
        MLCode()
        await module_client.send_message_to_output(msg,
                                                   "output1")
```

4. Create a message-receiving function:

```
def stdin_listener():
    while True:
        try:
            selection = input("Press Q to quit\n")
            if selection == "Q" or selection == "q":
                print("Quitting...")
                break
        except:
            time.sleep(10)
```

5. Start our message sender thread and our message receiver thread:

```
async def main():
    try:
        module_client = \
        IoTHubModuleClient.create_from_edge_environment()
        await module_client.connect()
        listeners = asyncio.gather(send_d2c_message(module_client))

        loop = asyncio.get_event_loop()
        user_finished = loop.run_in_executor(None, stdin_listener)

        # Wait for user to indicate they are done listening for
        # messages
        await user_finished

        # Cancel listening
        listeners.cancel()

        # Finally, disconnect
        await module_client.disconnect()

    except Exception as e:
        print ( "Unexpected error %s " % e )
        raise
```

6. Set the standard Python main program entry point:

```
if __name__ == "__main__":
    loop = asyncio.get_event_loop()
    loop.run_until_complete(main())
    loop.close()
```

How it works...

In this recipe, we learned how to prepare a device and development environment for developing an edge module that you can deploy your code on. The IoT Edge coding paradigm works on receiving messages, performing actions, and then sending messages. In the code for this recipe, we separated these actions into different tasks that can be run independently of each other. This allows us to perform actions such as getting and sending messages in a slow time loop and evaluating our data in a faster loop. To do this, we used `asyncio`, which is a library that facilitates multi-threading in Python. Once you have your code ready, you can build a Docker container and deploy that to other devices with the edge module installed or an entire fleet of devices. In the *There's more...* section, we will discuss how to do that.

There's more...

Now that you have added the code to the device, you will need to build the code locally on the device's architecture. Once you've ensured that the device image is working, you can upload it to your container registry. This ensures you have the devices within your IoT Hub. To do this, go into your Visual Studio project and right-click on the `module.json` file. A new context menu will appear that will allow you to either build locally or build and push to your container registry:

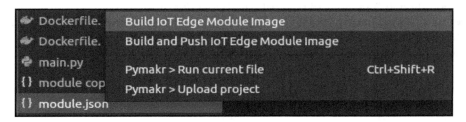

From here, you can create a deployment manifest by right-clicking on the `deployment.template.json` file and selecting **Generate IoT Edge Deployment Manifest**. VS Code will generate a `config` folder with a `deployment.arm32.json` file inside it:

Locate and right-click on the `deployemtn.arm32.json` file; a new context menu will appear that will allow you to deploy to a single device or a fleet of devices:

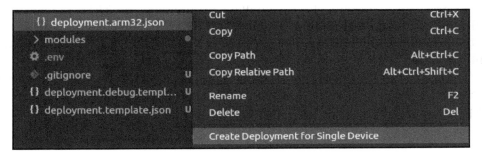

This very same menu allows you to also push to a fleet of devices. Once you've deployed your update, you can view the update in the portal. If you have that deployment update the device twins, you can use that to query the status of the deployments across your fleet.

Offloading to the web with TensorFlow.js

One of the biggest drivers of failures in IoT is cost. Often, devices are sold at a low fixed price and then have a reoccurring cost for the device manufacturer. There are multiple ways of reducing reoccurring costs. One of these is to offload some of the machine learning compute to the device or application accessing the data. In this recipe, we are going to use TensorFlow.js to offload the expensive compute to the browser of the person looking at the web page.

Getting ready

For this recipe, we are going to be building off of the *Implementing LSTM to predict device failure* recipe from `Chapter 4`, *Deep Learning for Predictive Maintenance*, where we looked at the NASA *Turbofan Run to Failure* dataset. You can find the Databricks notebooks in the repository for this chapter. For this recipe, we are going to be using the MLflow experiment to retrieve our model. We will convert that model into one that can be run on the frontend using TensorFlow.js. Before we get started with TensorFlow.js, you will need to run `pip install tensorflowjs`.

From there, you will need to find the model you downloaded from the MLflow artifact; that is, the saved Keras model. To do this, run the following command:

```
tensorflowjs_converter --input_format=keras model.h5 tfjs_model
```

Here, `model.h5` is the saved Keras LSTM model from the predictive maintenance dataset and `tfjs_model` is the folder that the model will be placed in.

From there, open Visual Studio. Here, we will be writing two files. The first will be an HTML file, while the second will be a JavaScript file. Once you've created these files, you can run them locally with the `webserver.py` file in the GitHub repository for this chapter. This will run your `index.html` file and any other files in your web browser at `http://localhost:8080/index.html`. Something else that's in the GitHub repository for this chapter is a `data.json` file that represents a web service where data is returned to the web page.

How to do it...

The steps for this recipe are as follows:

1. In the `index.js` file, add a `GetData` function that gets the data from `data.json`:

    ```
    async function GetData(){
    $.get( "/data.json", function( data ) {
    $( "#data" ).text( data["dat"] );
    predict(data["dat"])
    });
    }
    ```

2. Make a function that pulls in the model and evaluates the data:

    ```
    async function predict(dat)
    {
        const model = await
    tf.loadLayersModel('/tfjs_model/model.json');
        console.log(model)
        dat = tf.tensor3d(dat, [1, 50, 25] )
        dat[0] = null
        console.log(dat)
        var pred = model.predict( dat)
        const values = pred.dataSync();
        let result = "Needs Maintenance"
        if(values[0] < .8)
            result = "Does not need Maintenance"
        $('#needed').html(result )
    }
    ```

3. Create an `index.html` file that will call your `js` file:

    ```
    <!DOCTYPE html>
    <html>
    <head>
    <title>Model</title>
    <script
    src="https://cdn.jsdelivr.net/npm/@tensorflow/tfjs@1.0.0/dist/tf.mi
    n.js"></script>
    <script
    src="https://cdn.jsdelivr.net/npm/@tensorflow/tfjs-vis@1.0.2/dist/t
    fjs-vis.umd.min.js"></script>
    </head>
    <body>
        <button onclick="GetData()">Maintenance Needed</button>
    <textarea id="data" style="width:400px;height:400px;"></textarea>
    ```

```
<div id="needed"></div>
</body>
<script
src="https://ajax.googleapis.com/ajax/libs/jquery/3.4.1/jquery.min.
js"></script>
<script type="text/javascript" src="index.js"></script>

</html>
```

How it works...

In this recipe, we took a pre-trained model written for Python and, using a conversion utility, converted it into something that will work on the web. Then, we pulled in data from a web service and evaluated it against the machine learning model. Finally, we displayed the text `"Needs Maintenance"` when our machine learning model has 80% confidence that the Turbofan engine is nearing the end of its remaining useful life.

There's more...

In recent years, web browsers have taken on vastly increased functionality. One aspect of this is the ability to handle data and process it in the background. An example of this can be found in the GitHub repository for this book. It's called `Dexie` and shows an example of adding data to a browser's database. You can also use service workers in modern web browsers. **Service workers** are background jobs that can be run on web browsers in the background. They can even work when a page is not active.

Deploying mobile models

Many IoT scenarios require that you have a graphical user interface; that is, a high level of compute, Bluetooth, and Wi-Fi and a cellular network. Most modern cell phones have these. An inexpensive IoT device can talk to an app on a smartphone via Bluetooth and use that app to perform ML and talk to the cloud.

Using cell phones can cut the time to market for IoT devices. These devices can use a secure and easily updatable app to send data to the cloud. The portability of cell phones is an appeal but also a drawback. Having a device constantly communicating with the cloud can drain a cell phone's battery so that it lasts for as little as 8 hours. Because of this, companies often look to edge processing to perform compute tasks such as machine learning. This allows the device to send data less frequently.

How cell phones are used for IoT is ubiquitous. Companies such as Fitbit and Tile use low-power **Bluetooth Low Energy** (**BLE**) to send data to consumer cell phones. The IoT devices themselves can be low power and offload most of the work to the attached cell phones. Other devices, such as patient heart monitors, warehouse inventory tools, and voice-activated kiosks, can have dedicated smart devices designed specifically for the needs of the application.

In this recipe, we are going to show you how to use TensorFlow Lite on Android. We are going to learn how to use a simple Android kiosk keyword-activated application and deploy it to a device. We are then going to learn how to sideload it into a device.

Getting ready

In this recipe, we are going to create a simple Android Studio application and add machine learning code to it. For this, you will need to download and install Android Studio. From there, create a new project and follow these steps:

1. Upon opening Android Studio, from the **Start** menu, select **+ Start a new Android Studio project**:

2. Then, you will need to select a UI template. In this recipe, we are going to select an empty activity:

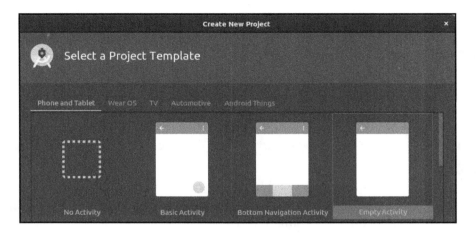

3. On the next screen, you will see a wizard that gives you the option to give the project a name and select a language for it. For this project, we will be selecting **Java** as our language:

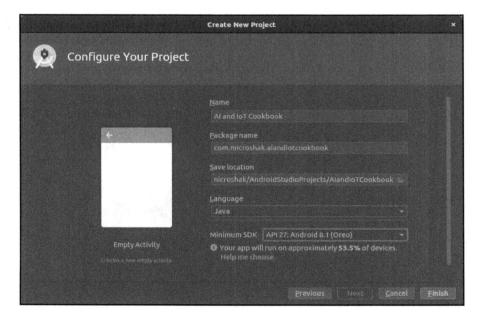

4. With that, a new project will open. Now, we need to import TensorFlow Lite into our project. To do this, go to the **build.gradle (Module: app)** section under **Gradle Scripts**:

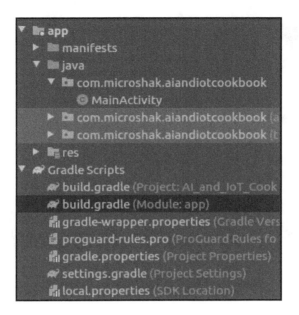

5. In the `build.gradle` JSON file under the `dependencies` section, add a reference to TensorFlow Lite (`implementation 'org.tensorflow:tensorflow-lite:+'`):

```
dependencies {
    implementation fileTree(dir: "libs", include: ["*.jar"])
    implementation 'androidx.appcompat:appcompat:1.1.0'
    implementation 'androidx.constraintlayout:constraintlayout:1.1.3'
    testImplementation 'junit:junit:4.12'
    androidTestImplementation 'androidx.test.ext:junit:1.1.1'
    androidTestImplementation 'androidx.test.espresso:espresso-core:3.2.0'
    implementation 'org.tensorflow:tensorflow-lite:+'
}
```

6. From there, in Android Studio, right-click on the **app** folder, select **New**, then select **Folder** and then **Assets folder**:

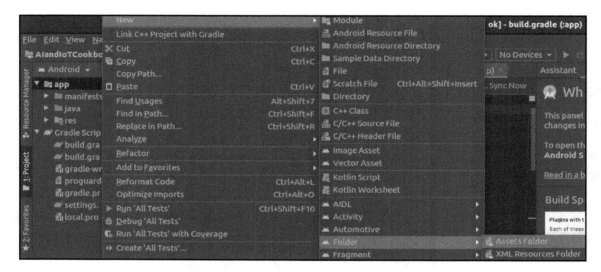

This is where we will put our trained model. Just as we used a `tfliteJS` conversion tool in the *Offloading to the web with TensorFlow.js* recipe, we can use the `tflite` conversion tool to convert our model.

How to do it...

The steps for this recipe are as follows:

1. In the header section of the `MainActivity.java` file, add the necessary reference to TensorFlow:

   ```
   import org.tensorflow.lite.Interpreter
   ```

2. In the `variables` section, initialize the `tflite` interpreter:

   ```
   Interpreter tflite;
   ```

3. In the `OnCreate` method, add the code that will load the model from the file into the `tflite` interpreter:

   ```
   tflite = new Interpreter(loadModelFile(activity));
   ```

4. Then, create a method that will load the model file:

```
private MappedByteBuffer loadModelFile(Activity activity) throws
IOException {
 AssetFileDescriptor fileDescriptor =
  activity.getAssets().openFd(getModelPath());
 FileInputStream inputStream = new
  FileInputStream(fileDescriptor.getFileDescriptor());
 FileChannel fileChannel = inputStream.getChannel();
 long startOffset = fileDescriptor.getStartOffset();
 long declaredLength = fileDescriptor.getDeclaredLength();
 return fileChannel.map(FileChannel.MapMode.READ_ONLY, startOffset,
                      declaredLength);
}
```

5. In a method that is called from a Bluetooth data feed, perform the necessary inference:

```
tflite.run(inputdata, labelProbArray);
```

How it works...

Similar to the *Offloading to the web with TensorFlow.js* recipe, this recipe takes in a TensorFlow Lite model, performs inference, and returns the probability. The TensorFlow Lite model works on small devices such as Android and can be used in applications and services.

Maintaining your fleet with device twins

A device twin is a set of tools designed to help us work with a fleet. They can be used to pass information down to a device, such as what model that device should be using. They can be used to pass more stateful information back to the cloud, such as the model's actual error rate.

Device twins have two sides. On the device side, there is a JSON file that acts like a writable configuration file, while on the cloud side, there is a writable database of properties. These two sides sync in an orderly way to allow you to reason about your fleet.

One advantage of a device twin is that you can see if model deployment actually worked. Often, machine learning models are updated with information changes, and new models are pushed down to the devices. These models can trigger out-of-memory exceptions and fail; they can also brick the device. Often, in an IoT product's life cycle, hardware may be substituted if a manufacture changes or certain components are no longer available.

Before we get started, we need to go over some basic concepts. We will do more of a deep dive on this topic in the *How it works...* section. A device twin consists of three parts:

- A **tags area**, which is responsible for generic tags such as the device's name, location, or owner. The tags area's data is set by the cloud.
- The next is the **desired properties**. The desired properties section is also set by the cloud. Conceptually, it is what state the cloud wishes the device to be in. This, for example, could be a model version or a threshold.
- The final property is a **reported property**. This property is set by the device. It can be a data value or the response to the desired property.

If, for example, the desired property or model version changes, we can attempt to update to the latest version and set our reported property to the desired version if the update worked. If it does not work, then we can query for that in the cloud. We can also use the tag section to update our devices in sets called **update rings**. We can use an update ring to obtain a rolling update, which allows us to update very few devices at first and multiple devices later. We can also use it to deploy different models depending on certain characteristics of a device, such as location and owner.

Getting ready

In this recipe, we are going to use Azure IoT Hub and Python. The Python version in our example needs to be above 3.6. We will need to install the following libraries:

```
pip3 install azure-iot-device
pip3 install asyncio
```

You will also need to get a device connection string from IoT Hub. In the *Setting up an IoT Hub* recipe of `Chapter 1`, *Setting Up the IoT and AI Environment*, we showed you how to set up IoT Hub in Azure. From there, you need to get a key for that individual device. To do this, navigate to the IoT Hub you created and click on the **IoT Devices** menu item in the left panel. Then, click the **+** button and add a device with symmetric key authentication:

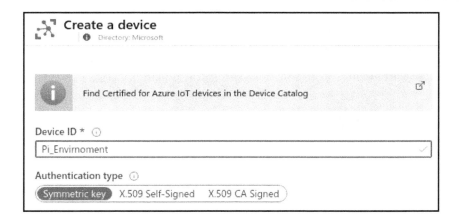

From here, you will see the device appear in the device list, as shown in the following screenshot. You can click on that item and get the device key:

You will also need to go into the shared access policy menu item and copy the service policy connection string. This connection string is for connecting to IoT Hub so that you can manage your fleet of devices. The previous key was for an individual device.

How to do it...

The steps for this recipe are as follows:

1. On the device side, import the necessary libraries:

```
import asyncio
from six.moves import input
from azure.iot.device.aio import IoTHubDeviceClient
```

2. Create a `main()` function and connect to the device:

```
async def main():
    device_client = \
    IoTHubDeviceClient.create_from_connection_string("Connection
                                                        String")

    await device_client.connect()
```

3. Create a twin listener:

```
def quit_listener():
    while True:
    selection = input("Press Q to quit\n")
    if selection == "Q" or selection == "q":
        print("Quitting...")
        break
```

4. Create a listen task:

```
asyncio.create_task(twin_patch_listener(device_client))
```

5. Listen for a quit signal:

```
loop = asyncio.get_running_loop()
user_finished = loop.run_in_executor(None, quit_listener)
```

6. Wait for the user finish signal and disconnect:

```
await user_finished
await device_client.disconnect()
```

7. Use `asyncio` to run the loop:

```
if __name__ == "__main__":
    asyncio.run(main())
```

8. On the cloud side (this is the computer helping you manage the fleet) use the following code to set the desired machine learning model version. First, import the necessary libraries:

```
import sys
from time import sleep
from azure.iot.hub import IoTHubRegistryManager
from azure.iot.hub.models import Twin, TwinProperties
```

9. Connect to IoT Hub with the service connection string:

```
iothub_registry_manager = \
IoTHubRegistryManager("Service Connection String")
```

10. Set the desired property so that it's the model version:

```
twin = iothub_registry_manager.get_twin("Device_id")
twin_patch = Twin( properties= \
TwinProperties(desired={'Vision_Model_Version' : 1.2}))
twin = iothub_registry_manager.update_twin(DEVICE_ID, twin_patch,
                                            twin.etag)
```

11. Later, in another Python file, we will query to see if the versions were updated. First, we import the necessary libraries:

```
import sys
from time import sleep
from azure.iot.hub import IoTHubRegistryManager
from azure.iot.hub.models import Twin, TwinProperties, \
QuerySpecification, QueryResult
```

12. We can then query for all of the devices with reported properties that do not match our desired properties:

```
query_spec = QuerySpecification(query="SELECT * FROM devices WHERE
properties.reported.Vision_Model_Version <> 1.2")
query_result = iothub_registry_manager.query_iot_hub(query_spec,
None, 100)
print("Devices that did not update: {}".format(',
'.join([twin.device_id for twin in query_result.items])))
```

How it works...

This recipe had three different code segments. The first was on the device side. This code gathers any changes that were made to the device via the device twin. In the next section, we instructed IoT Hub to update a reported property on a specific device. We then queried our fleet of devices and checked if all of our devices are updated to the model we wanted to use.

There's more...

A device twin is basically a large JSON file that resides on both the cloud and device side. It can be used to adjust settings, control the device, and set metadata about the device. There is another service that builds upon a device twin. It is called a **digital twin**. Digital twins have the same JSON file sync between devices and the cloud. They also have the additional benefit of connecting devices in a graph. A graph is a way of linking devices to each other. This can be done geographically. In other words, you can link devices by their locations. It can also link devices together locally. This is useful when you have devices that are related. A smart city, for example, would want devices that are related geographically. In this smart city, we would want to know if all the intersections in a geographic location had stopped traffic. In a factory, there could be manufacturing lines that contain related data. These manufacturing lines could contain dozens of IoT devices that provide different types of readings. Digital twins can help us diagnose problems with root cause analysis on slow assembly lines.

Enabling distributed ML with fog computing

Working in IoT generally means working with large data. Sensors can be verbose and the devices can be large as well. The CERN's particle accelerator, for example, generates over a petabyte a second. Sending this raw data to a central repository would be impractical. Many companies facing extremely large datasets or extremely fast-moving datasets can face challenges when it comes to dealing with their data.

In this recipe, we are going to distribute a workload across several systems, thereby allowing one system to take an image and another to process it. A small device, in our example, could take the image and stream it to an industrial PC or a set of servers in a factory. We are going to use `docker` and `docker-compose` here, while for our algorithm, we are going to use YOLO's (an image classification algorithm) OpenCV implementation.

Getting ready

This recipe will be quite verbose in terms of the amount of code we'll be seeing, but everything will be done in Docker. You can use VS Code's Docker extension to work directly within the Docker container. You will also need a device with a webcam attached to it. This could be a laptop or a Raspberry Pi with a webcam – it doesn't really matter. For this recipe, we are going to set up a machine learning service, a camera streaming service, and a service that allows the devices to know where other devices are, and allow you to view your classification across your entire fleet of devices.

Although this is fairly simple, listing the code for all of the containers would take dozens of pages. For the sake of brevity, in this recipe, we are going to show the computer vision module. The rest of the modules can be run using Docker and the code in the GitHub repository for this book.

How to do it...

The steps for this recipe are as follows:

1. On your compute device, download the machine learning model files for YOLO:

```
wget https://pjreddie.com/media/files/yolov3.weights
wget
https://raw.githubusercontent.com/microshak/AI_Benchtest_Device/yol
ov3.txt
wget
https://raw.githubusercontent.com/microshak/AI_Benchtest_Device/yol
ov3.cfg
```

2. Create a CPU folder and create an __init__.py file inside it:

```
from flask import Flask
cpu = Flask(__name__)

from CPU.Yolo import yolo
from CPU.manifest import manifest
cpu.register_blueprint(yolo)
cpu.register_blueprint(manifest)
```

3. Create a manifest.py file that will send the capabilities of the compute server to a centralized server:

```
from flask_apscheduler import APScheduler
from flask import Blueprint, request, jsonify, session
import requests
import socket
import json
import os
manifest = Blueprint('manifest','manifest',url_prefix='/manifest')
scheduler = APScheduler()

def set_manifest():
    f = open("manifest_cpu.json", "r")
    manifest = f.read()
    data = json.loads(manifest)
```

```
            data['host_name'] = socket.gethostname()
            gw = os.popen("ip -4 route show default").read().split()
            s = socket.socket(socket.AF_INET, socket.SOCK_DGRAM)
            s.connect((gw[2], 0))
            ipaddr = s.getsockname()[0]

            data['ip_address'] = ipaddr
            url = 'https://ai-benchtest.azurewebsites.net/device'
            r = requests.post(url = url, json =data)
            txt = r.text

        set_manifest()
        scheduler.add_job(id ='Scheduled task', func =set_manifest,
                        trigger = 'interval', minutes = 10)
        scheduler.start()
```

4. Create a `Yolo.py` file and import the necessary libraries:

```
        import cv2
        import pickle
        from io import BytesIO
        import time
        import requests
        from PIL import Image
        import numpy as np
        from importlib import import_module
        import os
        from flask import Flask, render_template, Response
        from flask import request
        import imutils
        import json
        import requests
        from flask import Blueprint, request, jsonify, session
```

5. Initialize the page as a Flask page:

```
        yolo = Blueprint('yolo', 'yolo', url_prefix='/yolo')
```

6. Initialize our drawing variables:

```
        classes = None
        COLORS = np.random.uniform(0, 300, size=(len(classes), 3))
```

7. Import the model class names:

```
        with open("yolov3.txt", 'r') as f:
            classes = [line.strip() for line in f.readlines()]
```

8. Create a helper function to get the output layers:

```
def get_output_layers(net):
    layer_names = net.getLayerNames()
    output_layers = [layer_names[i[0] - 1] for i in
                     net.getUnconnectedOutLayers()]
    return output_layers
```

9. Create a helper function that will draw a rectangle around the identified objects and insert the classification text:

```
def draw_prediction(img, class_id, confidence, x, y, x_plus_w,
                    y_plus_h):
    label = str(classes[class_id])
    color = COLORS[class_id]
    cv2.rectangle(img, (x,y), (x_plus_w,y_plus_h), color, 2)
    cv2.putText(img, label, (x-10,y-10), cv2.FONT_HERSHEY_SIMPLEX,
                0.5, color, 2)
```

10. Create a `Yolo` method that takes in an image and a neural network and then downscales the image:

```
def Yolo(image, net):
    try:
        Width = image.shape[1]
        Height = image.shape[0]
        scale = 0.00392

        blob = cv2.dnn.blobFromImage(image, scale, (416,416),
                                     (0,0,0), True, crop=False)
```

11. Set the image as the input on the neural network and perform the YOLO analysis:

```
        net.setInput(blob)
        outs = net.forward(get_output_layers(net))
```

12. Initialize the variables and set the confidence threshold:

```
        class_ids = []
        confidences = []
        boxes = []
        conf_threshold = 0.5
        nms_threshold = 0.4
```

13. Turn the machine learning result set into a set of coordinates we can apply to the image:

```
for out in outs:
    for detection in out:
        scores = detection[5:]
        class_id = np.argmax(scores)
        confidence = scores[class_id]
        if confidence > 0.5:
            center_x = int(detection[0] * Width)
            center_y = int(detection[1] * Height)
            w = int(detection[2] * Width)
            h = int(detection[3] * Height)
            x = center_x - w / 2
            y = center_y - h / 2
            class_ids.append(class_id)
            confidences.append(float(confidence))
            boxes.append([x, y, w, h])
```

14. Suppress any of our bounding boxes that do not meet the threshold criteria:

```
indices = cv2.dnn.NMSBoxes(boxes, confidences,
                           conf_threshold,
                           nms_threshold)
```

15. Get the bounding boxes and draw them inside the images:

```
for i in indices:
    i = i[0]
    box = boxes[i]
    x = box[0]
    y = box[1]
    w = box[2]
    h = box[3]
    draw_prediction(image, class_ids[i],
                    confidences[i], round(x),
                    round(y), round(x+w),
                    round(y+h))
```

16. Return the image:

```
return image
```

17. Create a function called `gen` that will import the model and continuously pull images from the camera device:

```
def gen(height,width, downsample, camera):

    net = cv2.dnn.readNet("yolov3.weights", "yolov3.cfg")
    while True:
        url = f'http://{camera}:5000/image.jpg?\
        height={height}&width={width}'
        r = requests.get(url) # replace with your ip address
        curr_img = Image.open(BytesIO(r.content))
```

18. Resize and color adjust the image:

```
        frame = cv2.cvtColor(np.array(curr_img), cv2.COLOR_RGB2BGR)
        dwidth = float(width) * (1 - float(downsample))
        dheight = float(height) * (1 - float(downsample))
        frame = imutils.resize(frame, width=int(dwidth),
                                height=int(dheight))
```

19. Perform the machine learning algorithm and stream back the results:

```
        frame = Yolo(frame, net)

        frame = cv2.imencode('.jpg', frame)[1].tobytes()
        yield (b'--frame\r\n'
                b'Content-Type: image/jpeg\r\n\r\n' +
                frame + b'\r\n\r\n')
```

20. Create a web address that will grab the URL parameters and put them through the algorithm:

```
@yolo.route('/image.jpg')
def image():

    height = request.args.get('height')
    width = request.args.get('width')
    downsample = request.args.get('downsample')
    camera = request.args.get('camera')

    """Returns a single current image for the webcam"""
    return Response(gen(height,width, downsample, camera),
                    mimetype='multipart/x-mixed-replace;
                    boundary=frame')
```

21. Back inside the root folder, create a `manifest.json` file that will broadcast the capabilities of the machine we are using:

```json
{
        "FriendlyName":"Thinkstation",
        "name":"Thinkstation",
        "algorithm":[{"name":"Object Detection"
                        ,"category":"objectdetection"
                        ,"class":"Computer Vision"
                        ,"path":"yolo/image.jpg"}
        ]
        , "ram":"2gb"
        , "cpu": "amd"
}
```

22. Create a `runcpu.py` file. This will be the file that starts the Flask server and registers the other code files:

```python
from os import environ
from CPU import cpu

if __name__ == '__main__':
    HOST = environ.get('SERVER_HOST', '0.0.0.0')
    try:
        PORT = int(environ.get('SERVER_PORT', '8000'))
    except ValueError:
        PORT = 5555
    cpu.run(HOST, PORT)
```

How it works...

This fog computing recipe shows how several different types of systems can be brought together to work as one. In this recipe, we showed the device code that grabs a video stream from a different system, perform a compute on it, and then passes it along to another system. Our final system in this case is a web application.

For different systems to communicate, there needs to be centralized state management. In this recipe, we used Flask and Redis. Every machine on our cluster registers its state and capabilities every 10 minutes. This allows the other machines to utilize machines that are on a network, thereby not bottlenecking on one machine. When a new machine comes online, it simply registers its state with our state server; as long as it keeps broadcasting, it is available to use.

There's more...

This recipe is dependent on other components. These components are in the GitHub repository for this chapter, under `AI_Benchtest`. You can start the programs by going into their respective folders and running `docker` or `docker-compose`. To run the camera server in a Terminal, go into the `AI_Benchtest_API` folder and run the following command:

```
docker-compose up
```

Next, you must run the `AI_Benchtest_Cam` module. In a Terminal, `CD` into the `AI_Benchtest_Cam` folder and run the same `docker-compose` command that you ran to get the API server running. At this point, both the camera and compute servers will be up and running and transmitting their status to the API server. Next, you will need to run a UI server so that you can give commands to the other servers. To do this, `CD` into the `AI_Benchtest_API` folder and run the following `docker` command to start the UI application:

```
docker build -t sample:dev . docker run -v ${PWD}:/app -v /app/node_modules
-p 3001:3000 --rm sample:dev
```

Packt.com

Subscribe to our online digital library for full access to over 7,000 books and videos, as well as industry leading tools to help you plan your personal development and advance your career. For more information, please visit our website.

Why subscribe?

- Spend less time learning and more time coding with practical eBooks and Videos from over 4,000 industry professionals

- Improve your learning with Skill Plans built especially for you

- Get a free eBook or video every month

- Fully searchable for easy access to vital information

- Copy and paste, print, and bookmark content

Did you know that Packt offers eBook versions of every book published, with PDF and ePub files available? You can upgrade to the eBook version at www.packt.com and as a print book customer, you are entitled to a discount on the eBook copy. Get in touch with us at customercare@packtpub.com for more details.

At www.packt.com, you can also read a collection of free technical articles, sign up for a range of free newsletters, and receive exclusive discounts and offers on Packt books and eBooks.

Other Books You May Enjoy

If you enjoyed this book, you may be interested in these other books by Packt:

Artificial Intelligence with Python Cookbook
Ben Auffarth

ISBN: 978-1-78913-396-7

- Implement data preprocessing steps and optimize model hyperparameters
- Delve into representational learning with adversarial autoencoders
- Use active learning, recommenders, knowledge embedding, and SAT solvers
- Get to grips with probabilistic modeling with TensorFlow probability
- Run object detection, text-to-speech conversion, and text and music generation
- Apply swarm algorithms, multi-agent systems, and graph networks
- Go from proof of concept to production by deploying models as microservices
- Understand how to use modern AI in practice

Hands-On Artificial Intelligence for Banking
Jeffrey Ng, CFA, Subhash Shah

ISBN: 978-1-78883-078-2

- Automate commercial bank pricing with reinforcement learning
- Perform technical analysis using convolutional layers in Keras
- Use natural language processing (NLP) for predicting market responses and visualizing them using graph databases
- Deploy a robot advisor to manage your personal finances via Open Bank API
- Sense market needs using sentiment analysis for algorithmic marketing
- Explore AI adoption in banking using practical examples
- Understand how to obtain financial data from commercial, open, and internal sources

Packt is searching for authors like you

If you're interested in becoming an author for Packt, please visit `authors.packtpub.com` and apply today. We have worked with thousands of developers and tech professionals, just like you, to help them share their insight with the global tech community. You can make a general application, apply for a specific hot topic that we are recruiting an author for, or submit your own idea.

Leave a review - let other readers know what you think

Please share your thoughts on this book with others by leaving a review on the site that you bought it from. If you purchased the book from Amazon, please leave us an honest review on this book's Amazon page. This is vital so that other potential readers can see and use your unbiased opinion to make purchasing decisions, we can understand what our customers think about our products, and our authors can see your feedback on the title that they have worked with Packt to create. It will only take a few minutes of your time, but is valuable to other potential customers, our authors, and Packt. Thank you!

Index

www.ingramcontent.com/pod-product-compliance
Lightning Source LLC
Chambersburg PA
CBHW060537060326
40690CB00017B/3515